HOAXES
THAT MADE
HEADLINES

Herma Silverstein
and Caroline Arnold

HOAXES
THAT MADE
HEADLINES

Julian Messner (M) New York

A Division of Simon & Schuster, Inc.

Published by Julian Messner, A Division of Simon & Schuster, Inc.
Simon & Schuster Building
Rockefeller Center
1230 Avenue of the Americas
New York, New York 10020
JULIAN MESSNER and colophon are trademarks of Simon & Schuster, Inc.
Manufactured in the United States of America

Library of Congress Cataloging-in-Publication Data

Silverstein, Herma.
    Hoaxes that made headlines.
    Bibliography: p.
    Includes index.
    Summary: Describes a variety of famous hoaxes and
deceptions in literature, music, art, science, and the
media. Also includes hoaxes meant as practical jokes.
    1. Impostors and imposture—Juvenile literature.
2. Deception—Juvenile literature. [1. Impostors and
imposture] I. Arnold, Caroline. II. Title.
HV6751.S55   1986   001.9′5   86-17986
ISBN 0-671-63259-0

With love to Ben and Larry,
my very own hoaxers who fool me every time.
                                        H.S.

For Art, Jennifer, and Matthew,
and with special thanks to Bill Mohrman.
                                        C.A.

CONTENTS

CHAPTER ONE

WHAT IS A HOAX?

Mundus vult decipi—ergo decipiatur.—The world wants to be fooled; therefore, it will be fooled.

—Sebastian Franck, 1533

The six conspirators sat silently in their private compartment as the train rattled its way from London to the port of Weymouth. The only woman in the group glanced at the men, who, like her, were dressed in long robes, turbans, and false beards, with dark stage makeup painted on their faces and hands. The woman shivered, although it was warm in the compartment. Fantasies of their dreadful fate, if their masquerade failed, whirled through her mind. Would she make a slip and give herself away as a woman, thereby exposing them all as the impostors they were?

The men sat stiff as mannequins, each lost in private thought. Would their ruse have been discovered by the time they reached Weymouth? Would the police meet them at the station, handcuffs ready to cart them off to prison? It seemed like idiocy to think they could fool the entire British navy.

The group's leader, Horace deVere Cole, wearing top hat and tails, and portraying a Foreign Office official escorting the entourage, had his own worries. Would the Swahili grammar

1

The "Abyssinian Princes," in all their finery, before embarking on their "Royal Visit" aboard Her Majesty's Flagship, the Dreadnought.

book he carried convince the naval officers that his "Ethiopian" speech was not, in fact, Latin gibberish? The entire plan depended upon exact timing and professional acting. If one person missed a cue, or broke character, their plan to show up the British navy as pompous stuffed-shirts would fail, and they would be hooted off the British Flagship *Dreadnought*.

Cole nodded to the others as the train hissed into the station. The woman, Virginia Stephen, later to become the celebrated novelist Virginia Woolf, checked her false beard. Then the group, which included Virginia's brother Adrian, followed her off the train.

Thus began what later became known as the *Dreadnought* Affair. Horace deVere Cole, famous for his practical jokes throughout London, conceived the idea of convincing the British navy that the Ethiopian Emperor and his entourage were paying an official visit to the *Dreadnought*. First Cole sent a telegram to the ship's Commander-in-Chief, announcing the Emperor's arrival, and signed the message with the name of the British Foreign Office chief.

When the impostors arrived in Weymouth, their anxiety disappeared as a naval officer in full ceremonial dress waited to drive them to the ship. Adrian Stephen later wrote, "We were almost acting the truth. It was hardly a question any longer of a hoax. Everyone was expecting us to act like the Emperor and his suite, and it would have been extremely difficult not to."

The Commander-in-Chief received them on board, and the group inspected a marine guard of honor, while the Commander explained the officers' different uniforms to Adrian Stephen who acted as interpreter. Stephen uttered some gibberish, hoping it sounded like Swahili. Fortunately for the impostors, nobody knew that Amharic is the language of Ethiopia, not Swahili. As Stephen continued to interpret, he became concerned that his phony Ethiopian would give them away. He decided to speak phrases from the Roman poet Virgil's *Aeneid*, mispronouncing the phrases just enough not to be recognizable as Latin. When he ran out of Virgil, he quoted the Greek poet Homer, making his "Swahili" believable by using the same phrase for a repeated situation. For example, each time the group had to duck through a doorway, a line from the *Aeneid* came to mean, "Watch your head, your Majesty."

Virginia Stephen, worried that her voice would give her away as a woman, motioned that she had a cold and said only,

"Chuck-a-choi, chick-a-choi" during the entire hoax.

Someone in the group started exclaiming "bunga, bunga" to show delight at whatever the Commander showed them. The other impostors caught on, and soon everyone was saying "bunga, bunga."

When it started to rain, the "Ethiopians" figured it was time to make a hasty exit before the rain washed off their makeup and peeled away their false beards. Stephen quickly interpreted a fond farewell to the Commander-in-Chief. Then the hoaxers boarded the launch for shore.

On the train back to London, Horace deVere Cole, forgetting the hoax was over, almost caused a minor insurrection by insisting the emperor could not sip his tea if the waiters did not wear white gloves to serve him. One of the waiters had to rush off the train when it stopped and buy gloves.

The imposturing Ethiopians agreed that the naval officers were so nice that they would not embarrass them by telling anyone about the hoax. Cole however, unable to resist the limelight, gave the story to the *Daily Express*. The paper carried a front page article about the *Dreadnought* hoax, which began: "Five young men and one young woman . . . perpetrated a most amazing and somewhat reprehensible practical joke on the Admiralty, the British Navy, and the H.M.S. *Dreadnought* in particular."

Other papers followed suit, and the *Daily Telegraph's* editorial claimed the admiral's courtesy had been abused, and that in sending a telegram under a false name, the group had committed an offense punishable by a fine or a year's imprisonment.

The result of this publicity forced the First Lord of the Admiralty to swear to the House of Commons that no flags had been hoisted, no salutes fired and no special train had been ordered for the "Ethiopians'" return to London.

The public, on the other hand, found the hoax amusing. The phrase "bunga, bunga!" caught on and became a catchall expression for the entire *Dreadnought* Affair. The Commander-in-Chief could not go anywhere without someone yelling "bunga, bunga!" at him. Horace deVere Cole was forever after known as the Prince of Practical Jokers.

Creating a Hoax

For centuries, people have been fooled by hoaxes such as the *Dreadnought* caper. Hoaxes are elaborate lies that are acted out rather than told. Some are perpetrated by an individual alone, but many are complicated, preplanned deceptions, requiring a cast of several people. The hoaxer thus sets up a sequence of events, in which the victim believes and then participates. As Norman Moss says in his book, *The Pleasures of Deception*, the hoaxer "invents a world, and persuades other people to live in it." Forged letters, diaries, and literary works; false newspaper reports; faked original works of art and musical compositions; imposture; and phony scientific discoveries have all played their part in hoaxes.

Hoaxes are conceived for many reasons—power, wealth, social position, revenge, fame, patriotism, hate, love, and often just for fun. Frequently a combination of motives encourages the hoaxer to carry out his or her deception. For instance, during World War II, Professor R. V. Jones, known at the time as one of the best practical jokers in England, switched from deceiving his friends to deceiving the Germans in order to help the Allies win the war.

Hoaxes have started wars and ruined reputations. In one instance, Premier Otto von Bismarck of Prussia, who became Chancellor of Germany, forged a report of a meeting between King William I of Prussia and the ambassador of France. Bismarck made the king appear to have insulted the ambassador. The angry French retaliated by attacking Prussia, and thus Bismarck provoked the Franco-Prussian War.

An often profitable type of hoax involves literary forgery. It is speculated that forgers have meddled with literature since the first Egyptian pharaoh put a seal on his writings. Even then, forgers lurked behind pyramids, waiting for the chance to melt the seal and alter the pharaoh's words. Forgers are people who invent or change the writings of others, then claim the falsified diary, letter, novel, play, or speech, is the genuine document.

One of the most popular forms of forgery is faking the signatures of famous people. Almost every important person in history has had his or her signature forged. The inveterate American forger, Arthur Sutton, imitated the signatures of such diverse figures as Sitting Bull, Richard Nixon, and Marilyn Monroe. Another famous forger, Joseph Cosey, added phony information to United States historical records from the time of Aaron Burr to Abraham Lincoln. One of the most prolific forgers of all time was Denis Vrain-Lucas from France, who forged more than twenty-seven thousand writings, including those of Judas Iscariot, Julius Caesar, and Charlemagne. He was finally caught when he mistakenly attributed the discovery of the laws of gravity to Pascal instead of to Isaac Newton.

Sometimes a talented writer, musician, or artist practices forgery by creating an original piece of work and then attributing it to the pen or paintbrush of a well-known person already established in that artistic field. In February, 1935, on his sixtieth birthday, the eminent violinist, Fritz Kreisler, confessed that for thirty years he had been playing his own works and crediting them to early masters such as Vivaldi, Couperin, and Pugnani. He claimed he had found the pieces hidden in old musical libraries and had made new arrangements of them. Kreisler explained that as a composer without an established reputation, he couldn't offer a program consisting entirely of his own compositions. He solved this by attributing them to others.

Other times authors write under an invented name or pseudonym. The American novelist Washington Irving wrote under the pseudonyms of Diedrich Knickerbocker, Geoffrey Crayon,

Jonathan Oldstyle, Launcelot Wagstaffe, and Friar Antonio Agapida. Nathaniel Hawthorne attributed his story *Rappacinni's Daughter* to a French writer named Audepine, which was French for Hawthorne's own name. The French author George Sand was really a woman named Amandine Aurore Lucie. She wrote from the 1830s until the 1860s, a time when it was considered to be unfeminine for a woman to be a professional writer. It was also considered unfeminine for women to go out at night unescorted, and she shocked Parisian society by donning men's clothes so she could attend the theater alone.

A hoax may also involve actually pretending to be another person. The first impostor may have been Jacob, who, according to the Old Testament, wore a goatskin to fool his blind father Isaac into believing he was his older brother Esau. Jacob wanted to gain Esau's inheritance. In colonial America, an indentured servant fooled people into believing she was a royal princess. A former Confederate soldier invented fake land grants made out in the names of fictitious Spanish ancestors, in order to claim ownership of the state of Arizona. Other impostors have assumed the roles of physicians, attorneys, teachers, and generals, among others.

History is frequently the victim of hoaxers. One of the most widely known fake histories concerns George Washington's chopping down his father's cherry tree. Citizens of Fredericksburg, Virginia, can take you to the *exact* spot where the nation's first President supposedly "never told a lie" when his father inquired whether he was responsible for cutting down the tree. For more than a century after this incident allegedly occurred, the story was taught to elementary school students as fact.

The origin of the cherry tree tale has now been traced to Dr. James Beattie, who included it in his book *The Minstrel*, published in 1799. The story later appeared in the fifth edition of *The Life of George Washington*, by Parson Lock Weems, who plagiarized Beattie's version.

Even the Declaration of Independence has not been immune

to accusations of forgery. According to citizens of Charlotte, North Carolina, the true declaration of America's independence is the *Mecklenburg Declaration*, a document containing five resolutions of independence from England. This document was supposedly adopted by North Carolinians at a meeting held on May 20, 1775, in Mecklenburg County, Charlotte, North Carolina.

In 1800, at another meeting held in Mecklenburg County, John M. Alexander, recording secretary, allegedly wrote the five resolutions from memory of the draft written in 1775. The Mecklenburg Declaration was never seen in print, however, until the *Raleigh Register*, a Charlotte newspaper, printed the five resolutions on the front page of its April 30, 1819, edition. Thomas Jefferson angrily denied the authenticity of the Mecklenburg Declaration, in spite of many people who came forward to testify that they had witnessed the Declaration's adoption.

Supposedly after its adoption, the document was sent to England by then North Carolina governor, Josiah Martin. The President of the United States at the time, James K. Polk, ordered an ambassador in England to search for the mysterious declaration. The ambassador never found a Mecklenburg Declaration in England's archives or anywhere else.

One famous attempt to prove the Declaration's authenticity was made by *Colliers* Magazine. This periodical printed a copy of the alleged front page of the June 3, 1775, edition of a newspaper called the *Cape Fear Mercury*, that was published when the Mecklenburg Declaration was supposedly adopted. The *Mercury* had allegedly printed the Mecklenburg's five resolutions on its front page.

Both the Carolina Historical Commission's secretary and the Library of Congress' manuscripts division chief exposed the *Colliers* copy of the newspaper as a fraud by showing that the type was not the same as that on genuine copies of the *Mercury*. Moreover, June 3, 1775, the date printed on the alleged front page of the newspaper, was not a Friday as printed. Further-more, the *Cape Fear Mercury* went out of business before 1775.

In spite of evidence against the Declaration's authenticity, the five resolutions are engrafted on North Carolina's statute books and state seal, along with the May 20, 1775, date of the alleged adoption of the Mecklenburg Declaration. May 20 is still declared a holiday in Charlotte.

Practical jokes are the simplest and most common of hoaxes. Almost everyone has played a practical joke on someone else. Identical twins often pretend to be each other in order to fool their teachers, friends, and in some cases, even their families. Seasoned summer campers are experts at fooling uninitiated cabin mates by telling them phony camp legends about mad-men, mysterious ghosts, and monsters lurking in the forests or mountains nearby. College students are also well known for perpetrating practical jokes, such as registering the dormitory dog for classes as a bona fide student. Student editors have printed false news items in university newspapers, fooling faculty and administrators into believing in fictitious founders of the campus, or national heroes.

Playing jokes just for fun is celebrated each year on April First—April Fools' Day. When the *Madison Capital Times* published a "photograph" of the state capitol's dome tumbling down on April 1, 1933, many readers failed to read the small print saying "April Fool." According to the article which accom-panied the picture, the explosion causing the disaster was the result of too much hot air generated by the state legislature!

Why People Fall for Hoaxes

Some hoaxes succeed because the opinions of "experts" put pressure on the victim to accept what he or she believes is false. This pressure to conform to group opinion overrules the vic-

April Fool's Joke, 1933, in Madison, Wisconsin.

tim's good sense and reasoning ability. It is very difficult for someone who does not know for sure that he or she is being fooled to insist upon his or her own opinions against the collective beliefs of many, no matter how erroneous those beliefs.

Experiments have proved that practically anyone can be fooled. In one case, a teacher sprayed pure water in his classroom and instructed the students to raise their hands when they smelled an odor. Seventy-three percent raised their hands. When 381 children were shown a toy camel and told they would see it move when a windlass turned, seventy-six percent said they saw the camel move. In another case a psychologist passed a foreign coin around a classroom of forty-eight boys. An hour later, he asked each student to draw a picture of the coin, showing the location of the hole in it. All but four boys drew the hole, even though there was no hole in the coin at all.

Frequently people make false assumptions about others based upon misleading evidence, such as the person's clothes, manners, and speech. Thus a man arriving at an expensive restaurant in a chauffeured limosine might be judged to be reasonably wealthy, well educated, and the manager or owner of a business. Hoaxers often use this tendency people have to make false conclusions to their own advantage. Therefore, a hoaxer proclaiming to be a baron from Italy has a better chance of fooling others if he dresses the part by wearing fashionable clothes, eats at fancy restaurants, and drives a sleek, expensive car.

A common motive for hoaxes is money. Many people are taken in by Get Rich Quick Schemes, or the hope that they might get something for nothing. They are easy targets for creative but unscrupulous business people. For example, each year, thousands of innocent people lose large sums of money by buying fake oil wells, gold mines, or stock certificates. Hoaxes for profit such as these are criminal offenses and are punishable by law.

Many times people fall for a hoaxer's tale because they want it to be true. The perpetrators of the forged Hitler diaries took advantage of the fact that original Hitler memorabilia hold a certain attraction for many people. For years many forged paintings, photographs and poems of Adolf Hitler have come out of East Germany.

On one occasion an alleged baby picture of Hitler caused a

Adolf Hitler.

sensation in Westport, Connecticut. Acme Newspictures, Inc., in May 1938, reissued a baby picture of Hitler with this caption: "Still unexplained after nearly four years is the mystery of the hoax through which an unauthentic picture of Adolf Hitler as a baby was circulated through the United States."

The German consul labeled the photograph in 1933 as a "fabrication" and said it had been printed in the United States. Inquiry showed the photo had, in fact, originated in Austria and somehow mysteriously arrived in the United States.

The plot thickened when Mrs. Harriet M. W. Downs of Westport, Connecticut, happened to glance through a popular magazine and recognized the Hitler photograph as one of her son, John May Warren, taken when he was two years old. The original snapshot had been retouched so that a baby cap was painted out, and what had been little John's babyish squint into the sun in the original, was now distorted to appear as a grimace in the face.

Yet, with all this evidence, there was still no explanation as to how the photograph got from America to Austria in the first place, nor any clue as to who conceived the hoax and why.

Perpetrators of hoaxes seem to enjoy the challenge of testing the public's credulity. Detecting the difference between the real and the fabricated is often difficult, and many hoaxers succeed because they are able to approximate the truth so closely that only experts can unmask them.

The details of how people have managed to fool the public and often even the experts have traditionally provided newspapers and magazines with stories and headlines that attract readers. Everyone wants to know the secrets as to how the experts can be fooled, even if only for a moment. As the philosopher Plato wrote over two thousand years ago, "Whatever deceives seems to produce a magical enchantment."

CHAPTER TWO

THE FAKE HITLER DIARIES

The long-awaited offensive has begun. May the Lord God stand by us.

These are the last words in the recently unearthed Adolf Hitler diaries. During the final days of World War II, while the Allies prepared to storm Berlin, the Führer hid in his underground bunker and supposedly scribbled in his diary. This last entry is dated April 16, 1945. Fifteen days later, Adolf Hitler is said to have pointed a pistol at his head and shot himself. But did Hitler really write these words? Did he keep a diary at all?

In April, 1945, on Hitler's orders, German officials scrambled to hide war documents that, if discovered by the enemy, would provide the evidence to charge the Führer and his Nazi accomplices with committing war crimes. Nazi officials stripped the Berlin bunker of Hitler's secret documents, correspondence, and gold bullion, then packed the incriminating evidence inside a steel case. They loaded the case onto one of ten small airplanes carrying Hitler's staff and important cargo to his pre-arranged hideout in Bavaria. Supposedly Hitler's diary, hand-written by the Führer between 1932 and 1945, and totalling sixty-two volumes the size of magazines and bound in imitation-leather covers, was one of the items packed inside the case. En route to Bavaria, the plane crashed in what is now East Germany. All the cargo was destroyed except, apparently, the steel case.

One account claims that a German soldier salvaged the case from the burning wreckage. Another tale insists some farmers living nearby rescued the box. Both versions, however, allege that the diaries were then hidden in a hayloft, where they remained untouched and unread for nearly forty years.

On April 22, 1983, Gerd Heidemann, a reporter for the West German magazine *Stern*, startled the world with an incredible announcement. He said he had acquired the secret, long-lost Hitler diaries. Heidemann, then fifty-one, was a specialist in Nazi memorabilia. He claimed a German dealer in Nazi arti-facts had obtained the Hitler diaries and offered to sell him the volumes.

So great was *Stern*'s desire to own the diaries that the editors gave Heidemann 3.75 million dollars to purchase them, even though he refused to identify the artifacts dealer or the circum-stances surrounding the discovery of the diaries. In addition, two months before Heidemann went public with his news, *Stern* offered serialization rights to other publications, who jumped at the chance to print a journalistic scoop. *Stern* received a total of three million dollars from these publications, which included *Newsweek*, *Life*, the London *Sunday Times*, the *New York Post*, and the *Star*, a Los Angeles, California-based weekly. Rupert Murdoch, a media magnate whose organization owns both the London *Times* and *Sunday Times* and the *New York Post*, paid four hundred thousand dollars to *Stern* for British commonwealth rights.

Reporter Gerd Heidemann displaying three of sixty-two alleged diaries of late German dictator Adolf Hitler.

When Heidemann first made his claim, many historians rejoiced. Finally they would know the truth about Adolf Hitler, who was perhaps the most evil man in history. Historians realized that if the diaries were authentic the entire history of World War II might have to be rewritten. After the initial announcement, however, support gradually fell away. More and more people questioned the authenticity of the diaries. Then, only two weeks after the diaries were revealed, the scholars' bubble burst. On May 6, historical authorities and handwriting experts cried "hoax."

The first thing that was pointed out was that even though the 1945 plane crash had been verified, the condition of the wreckage had not. Two survivors of the crash, the only witnesses, had since died. Critics further noted that after the July 20, 1944, assassination attempt on Hitler, his writing arm was known to be partially paralyzed. Yet, according to the diary entry for that same afternoon, Hitler purportedly wrote: "I am OK. Only got a few bruises. I was blown up against the ceiling together with the table top. I am speaking later today to the nation over all transmitters."

Backing up their skepticism with documented facts about the Führer's personal habits, the historians stressed that there was no evidence that Hitler ever kept a diary or showed the slightest interest in doing so. In the millions of words written about him in authenticated biographies, court documents, and interviews with hundreds of his closest associates and servants, there was not one reference to the diary. His former aides claim the only time they heard the Führer mention a diary was to express his disdain for people who kept them. His staff was with him every waking hour, even eating meals with him. If Hitler had kept a diary, his aides would have known about it.

Historians knew also that it would be easy to gather the material to forge a diary. Hitler had no qualms about people taking down his dinnertime conversation, which included anecdotes about his childhood and feelings about world leaders and government in general. Many of these have already been published, and a forger would have easy access to the information in order to alter it, add a few invented anecdotes of his or her own, and thereby make the diary sound authentic. No one but Hitler would have known what private feelings he had written in his diary. Even so, in the alleged diaries, there is a striking lack of Hitler's personal emotions.

Furthermore, critics pointed out that Hitler hated to write. He suffered from palsy and dictated everything to his secretary, including his book *Mein Kampf*. It is a documented fact that shortly before Hitler committed suicide, his mind was so tormented that his hands shook terribly. Apparently, he could not even pick up a glass of water without spilling it all over himself.

Another fact the forgers overlooked in their Hitler homework was that the dictator had expensive tastes and normally used stationery imprinted with eagles and swastikas. Yet the alleged diaries were written on cheap notebook paper and bound in imitation leather. "Cheap leather!" exclaimed Hitler's former air force adjutant, Colonel Nicolaus von Below. "Hitler would have had real leather or nothing at all."

Charles Hamilton, a New York autograph dealer, took one look at photocopies of the volumes and said, "I could have done better myself." He claimed the entire "look" of the diaries was faulty. Comparing an alleged 1938 diary entry to the writing in Hitler's will, known to be one of the few genuine Hitler handwriting specimens, Hamilton said: "Hitler's actual script is nervous and impetuous. He bears down heavily on the pen. The words sweep forcefully across the page and plunge head-long downhill at the end of the line, as if they can hardly keep up with the torrent of his thoughts."

Hamilton claimed the forger had not put enough hard pressure on his pen. "Hitler bore down, and his 'e's' and 'A's' close up with ink. [The forger] looks like he is tiptoeing through the tulips when he should be driving forward with a spear."

Often the first clues of forgery that handwriting analysts look for when examining a possibly fraudulent document are alphabet letters printed alike over many lines and over different periods of time. Forgers usually learn other people's formation of alphabet letters individually, so that they end up writing every letter in a fake document identically. People change how they write individual letters depending upon how they feel that day, their writing posture, and even how they feel about what they are writing. As FBI special Agent James Lile says, "Your signature on a $50,000 mortgage is a little more careful than on a $10 check."

Hamilton noted upon further examination of the Hitler diaries, that the individual letters were written almost identically in every entry. Another obvious clue to the diaries being fraudulent, Hamilton said, was how "schoolbookish the writing appears, how measured it is, how the ink is not distributed evenly over the strokes"—as if whoever wrote it took pains to carefully form each letter. "It screams of forgery," he added.

As the furor over the diaries' authenticity rose to an international debate, *Newsweek* magazine, which had planned to print excerpts from the volumes, called in handwriting consultant Kenneth Rendell. Rendell is an historical expert who has bought and sold hundreds of genuine Adolf Hitler documents. *Stern* editor Peter Koch allowed Rendell to examine the first and last volumes.

Rendell immediately found the diaries amateurish and crude with every Hitler signature badly written. "I felt like a well-conditioned athlete who wins because the other competitors fail to show up," he said about his extensive preparation to examine the volumes.

Rendell discovered additional flaws such as pages filled with cursive "a's" even though Hitler usually *printed* capital "A's." The crossbar on the "f" of Hitler's genuine "Adolf" slants from the upper left to the lower right, whereas the crossbar in the diary signatures slanted from the lower left to the upper right. Furthermore, the dictator's "E's" usually curled upward; the Heidemann diaries cut straight across. Hitler wrote a simple "K", using sharp strokes; the diary "K's" were printed in an

Adolf Hitler's genuine signature, probably written in 1932.

Adolf Hitler's genuine signature, probably written in 1939.

elegant manner. Hitler, like most people, used a more simple style for writing text than he did for writing his signature; the diary entries used the signature-type style every time. The Führer's real signature also changed throughout the years, becoming smaller and more cramped as his health deteriorated, whereas his signature in the alleged diaries grew from being tightly written in the early entries, to open and flamboyant toward the end.

Also, according to German historian, Werner Maser, Hitler's palsy eventually forced him to write only in pencil, so that his trembling hand would not smear ink all over the pages. Yet, the alleged diaries switch from pen to pencil and back to pen.

Moreover, in 1945, when writing in pencil, Hitler would have used a pencil that showed a dull mark whenever it needed sharpening; the diary entries in pencil are all sharp, causing speculation that the forger used a mechanical pencil. Mechanical pencils were not invented until after the war. Chemical analysis of the bindings and the glue on the labels showed they contained polyester threads, which were not manufactured until after World War II. The ink and the imitation-leather covers were produced after 1945, and the paper contained postwar whitening agents made after 1955.

Additional evidence indicating the diaries were forged was discovered by inspecting the typeset used to print the labels. Old typewriters have their own fingerprints in their tilted, offset letters. Inspection of the typeset proved that the typewriter used to print the labels was a 1925 model. Tests comparing labels typed in 1932 to those typed in 1945 showed that the same typewriter was used to print the labels on all sixty-two volumes. Yet there had been no evident wear on the typewriter keys, indicating that the labels had been typed all at once, rather than over a thirteen-year time span.

Professor Horst Heiderhoff, an expert on graphics, found a shocking flaw in the elaborate metal initials used on the cover of one volume. The "A" in Hitler's initials "A. H." was turned into an "F", in a typeface called Engraver's Old English. Yet, the Nazis had banned this typeface in the 1940s because they considered it "Jewish".

Kenneth Rendell also found that none of the words was blotted—a careless attitude not expected from the Führer. This indicated that the ink used was not from a fountain pen, which would have required words to be blotted to prevent smudges. Most likely a ballpoint pen had been used, which in 1945 was not yet invented.

Numerous historical errors throughout the text also shouted "forgery." Whoever wrote the diaries obviously had not re-searched wartime history well enough. For example, the diary talks about the half million people who showed up at a Hitler rally in Breslau, whereas in reality around 130,000 people attended. Another entry describes General Franz Ritter Von Epp congratulating Hitler in 1937 on his fiftieth anniversary in army service. At the time the Führer was only forty-eight years old. Historians say it was Hitler who praised Von Epp for *his* fifty years in the Army.

Throughout the volumes, there were no changes in the text—no words were crossed out or erased. Most people make at least one or more errors in writing any composition and have to erase or scratch out. Yet the alleged Hitler volumes appeared as if Hitler knew ahead of time just what he wanted to write and never changed his mind. In addition, the volumes supposedly lay in a hayloft for forty years, yet none of the pages was stained or worn.

Besides well-documented, technical facts that repudiated the diaries' authenticity, doubts about Gerd Heidemann's honesty as a reporter fed the flames of forgery as well. Four years earlier, Heidemann had claimed to have discovered secret letters between World War II Italian dictator Benito Mussolini and then British Prime Minister Winston Churchill. British historian David Irving examined the letters at the time and branded them forgeries.

Heidemann's character itself, which leaned toward Nazi doctrines, also made him suspect. Historian Werner Maser described Heidemann as "gullible, and morbidly interested in Nazi paraphernalia." Heidemann supposedly kept what he believed to be Hitler's uniform in the trunk of his car. High on the guest list at Heidemann's wedding were two former Nazi generals who served as witnesses to the marriage. According to Maser, Heidemann once "was furious" at Maser and accused him of smearing the Führer's name by writing in a book review that Hitler had been aware of the mass murder of Jews, and had even ordered that the killing should be speeded up.

A statement made by Heidemann's wife Gina gave credence to his growing reputation as a Nazi aficionado. After officials at *Stern* questioned Heidemann for hours about how he obtained the diaries and then decided to cancel the entries' publication in their magazine, Gina said, "It's terrible. But no matter what happens, we will always believe in the diaries." She accused the people who declared the volumes forgeries as trying to "suppress the truth," adding, "It would have been a joy to tell the reality about the Führer."

The few people who believed the diaries were authentic did so partly because they wished them to be. There has always been a fascination with Hitler memorabilia. Countless bestsellers about the Führer, from thriller novels to psychoanalytic reviews, regularly spin off the presses. Some books, such as historian John Toland's *Adolf Hitler*, William Shirer's *The Rise and Fall of the Third Reich*, and Albert Speer's *Inside the Third Reich*, continue to sell thousands of copies year after year. Hitler has been portrayed in motion pictures many times, including memorable performances by silent film star Charlie Chaplin in *The Great Dictator* (1943), by Alec Guinness in *Hitler: The Last Ten Days* (1973), and by Peter Sellers in *The Undercover Hero* (1975).

With the exception of Abraham Lincoln, Hitler's signature

has been forged more times than any other person's. A genuine Hitler signature brings a high price in the Nazi memento marketplace. For instance, a genuinely inscribed, two-volume first edition of *Mein Kampf* can sell for ten thousand dollars, and a handwritten letter from Hitler to a top Nazi leader can cost as much as twenty-five thousand.

John Toland offered another explanation besides monetary gain for the world's continued interest in Hitler, thus giving a possible reason why *Stern* bought the alleged diaries so quickly, without first checking the volumes' authenticity: "In movies and plays the most fascinating characters are villains. Drama is conflict, and Hitler gave a horrible, but immensely dramatic, show. We are eager to believe something like these diaries could exist. They could bring us close to the man who changed all our lives."

It was on April 25, three days after Heidemann's announcement, that the London *Sunday Times* printed the first excerpt from the alleged diaries. On May 2, British historian David Irving, who had challenged the diaries' authenticity from the outset, changed his mind and supported the authenticity of the diaries. He said that in 1982 a former archivist of the Nazi Party, August Priesack, had offered him a portion of a diary supposedly written by Hitler. After examining it, Irving pronounced the diary a forgery. When *Stern* representatives showed him excerpts from the diaries, Irving at first said he believed the *Stern* excerpts and the one he examined the previous year came from the same source.

Then Irving read excerpts from the entries in the last volumes, and announced, "I'm becoming more inclined to believe they are authentic." Irving said what convinced him was that the handwriting in the later diaries "sloped down off the rulings," due to Hitler's suffering from Parkinson's disease, and it was unlikely that a forger would have known about Hitler's affliction.

Irving had initially informed the *Sunday Times* that the diaries were forgeries. Even so, in February, 1983, *Times* Newspapers still paid one million pounds (about 1.55 million American dollars) for the excerpt rights. In its April 25 edition, the rival *Sunday Mail* said, "The so-called private diaries of Adolf Hitler could well turn out to be the most outrageous literary hoax of all time."

Practically within twenty-four hours, Lord Bullock, a distinguished British historian, reacted to the *Mail*'s editorial by asking that an international commission of inquiry investigate the diaries' authenticity. On May 3, to counter the growing number of skeptics, *Stern* hired its own authorities to compare Hitler's writing on documents that were assumed to be genuine with six pieces of paper supposedly written by Hitler and obtained at the same time. *Stern*'s analysts reported that the handwritings matched.

Kenneth Rendell claimed they matched because the samples were also fakes, as they had been supplied by Gerd Heidemann. Therefore the experts were comparing forgeries to forgeries.

The next day, May 4, *Stern*'s editorial board ordered that some of the volumes be examined by West Germany's Federal Archives in Coblenz. Only the magazine's Editor-in-Chief, Peter Koch, refused to stop defending the Hitler diaries as genuine. While the Federal Archives checked the diaries' authenticity, Koch flew to New York with the first and last volumes and displayed them on national television. He said: "I expected the uproar and expected that many incompetent people would denounce the diaries as fakes. This is because every other publishing house will envy our story and every historian will envy us."

On May 6, a news conference was held by West Germany's Interior Minister, Friedrich Zimmermann, and Federal Archives President, Hans Booms. Zimmerman announced that "the Federal Archives is convinced the documents they were given were not produced by Hitler's hand, but were written in the postwar period." Hans Booms called the diaries a "blatant, grotesque, and superficial forgery." He claimed that a portion of the entries was plagiarized from former Nazi Federal Archivist Max Domarus' book, published in 1962, entitled, *Hitler's Speeches And Proclamations, 1932–45*. Domarus made many errors in his text, and Booms noted that, "where Domarus makes a mistake, the forger makes a mistake. Where Domarus keeps silent, the forger keeps silent."

Newsweek magazine's former staffer James P. O'Donnell found similarities between the diaries and his own book, entitled *The Bunker*. A copy of *The Bunker* had been given to Heidemann by former SS Major General Wilhelm Mohnke, the last commander of Hitler's Berlin bunker, to thank Heidemann for cruises on his yacht.

As often happens with hoaxes that make headlines, copycat deceptions occurred. A supposed expert called *Newsweek* from a New York City phone booth to expose the entire fraud. "*I* have Hitler's diaries," he exclaimed.

After the Hitler diaries were officially declared a hoax, Gerd Heidemann was arrested for fraud, subsequently naming Konrad Kujau, then a forty-six-year-old confidence trickster, as the artifacts dealer who had sold him the alleged diaries. Kujau immediately fled Germany but was later caught at a Bavarian border station where he was arrested as an accomplice.

Henri Nannen, *Stern*'s publisher, stated, "We have reason to be ashamed. We are going to uncover the full story of this forgery and lay it before our readers." The staff at the magazine called the diaries, "the most expensive waste-paper collection in the world." The first fallout from the hoax was editor Peter Koch's resignation. Running a close second, was the loss of three million dollars and *Stern*'s damaged reputation.

Hugh Trevor-Roper, a Cambridge historian, and author of a highly acclaimed book, *The Last Days of Hitler*, suffered a dent in his reputation as well. Early on in the whole affair he had examined the volumes in a Swiss bank and declared: "When I turned the pages of those volumes, my doubts gradually dissolved. I am now satisfied they are authentic." However, when debates about the diaries' legitimacy rose to an international level, Trevor-Roper qualified his statement, admitting that "some documents in that collection were forgeries" and that more examination of the documents would be needed to verify their authenticity.

At the trial held in September, 1984, in Hamburg, Germany, Kujau insisted he was a go-between in the fraud. He said he had secured the diaries from relatives in East Germany, who had obtained the volumes from the farmers who hid them in their hayloft in 1945. Kujau named his brother, a major general in the East German army, and his brother-in-law, the director of a museum, as these relatives. Heidemann alleged he himself obtained the diaries from a senior official in communist East Germany.

Klaus Oldenhage, the second-ranking official at the Federal Archives, said, "The East German government was not involved, in my opinion. I don't believe that a government agency would have done such a bad job."

Testimony in the trial revealed that Kujau's brother was in reality a reserve East German policeman and railway porter, and his brother-in-law, a hospital heating maintenance man. Neither was involved in the forgeries. An independent investigation by *Stern* showed that Kujau's handwriting matched the handwriting in the diaries. The artifacts dealer finally confessed to having forged the entire sixty-two volumes.

The trial progressed, at times seeming to reflect the same amateurish style that characterized the hoax itself. One of the seven judges kept falling asleep in the courtroom until he had to be replaced. Most of the testimony was received by outbursts of laughter from the stands, prompting the chief judge, Hans-Ulrich Schroeder, to issue so many rebukes that he finally exclaimed, "This is not a theatrical performance. It is a legal proceeding. Occasional joviality can be permitted, but I request a bit of restraint."

From the minute Kujau entered the courtroom carrying two sketches of nude women, signed "A. Hitler," he continually caused a scene. When a reporter asked Kujau if he planned to forge more diaries, he responded, "Of course. I've got to make a living." He expressed contempt for the "Hitler experts" who judged his forged Hitler diaries authentic. When an historian pronounced the diaries authentic on television, Kujau felt as though he had been "hit by a train." He compared the experts' gullibility to another occasion when he fooled a Munich art expert by easily pawning off a fake painting by Hitler of his mistress Eva Braun. "Some art dealer," Kujau scoffed. "That painting wasn't ten days old." Kujau admitted he copied sections of the last Hitler volumes from newspaper articles dealing with the end of the war.

Eleven years before, Heidemann had sold his house to buy a yacht supposedly once owned by Hermann Goering, former Nazi chief of the German air force. When Heidemann heard that Goering had buried treasure in an East German lake, he invested thousands of dollars in a fruitless treasure hunt. Heidemann testified that he had believed Kujau's tale about high-ranking East German figures who were being paid off to smuggle the diaries, hidden in pianos, into the West. At one point, Heidemann said he asked Kujau if he could ship the diaries in ten pianos simultaneously. Manfred Bissinger, former deputy chief editor of *Stern*, said, "It was always typical for Gerd Heidemann to believe the craziest, most improbable stories."

Although Heidemann swore he always trusted the diaries' authenticity, Kujau said Heidemann saw him seal some volumes with a fake stamp. The reporter even once paid Kujau between one and two hundred thousand dollars for purported signatures of Frederick the Great, George Washington, and letters written by Napoleon to Josephine. In 1981, Heidemann asked Werner Maser to authenticate a gun he had purchased. The gun was supposedly the one Hitler used to commit suicide—a 7.65 Walther pistol. Maser told Heidemann that there was "a whole suitcase full of Hitler suicide guns, all forged with Hitler's initials and the correct certificate number."

As more evidence was revealed, people were shocked that a respected magazine such as *Stern* had fallen for such a poorly executed hoax. Hans Bremmer, the magazine's political editor said, "We made mistakes, embarrassing ones. If our editors had worked well as editors, it wouldn't have happened. It was generally sloppy work."

On July 9, 1985, in Hamburg, West Germany, after a trial that lasted eleven months, the jury found Gerd Heidemann and Konrad Kujau guilty of fraud. Heidemann was sentenced to four years, eight months in prison, and Kujau to four years, six months. Even while the defendants listened to the foreman of the jury read the verdict, the two men still claimed they were innocent. Each swore the other had tricked him about the diaries' origins and the money paid for them. Both Heidemann and Kujau were charged with collecting 3.1 million dollars from *Stern* magazine for the sixty fake Hitler volumes. At the time of the trial, most of the payoff money had not been recovered.

After Judge Hans-Ulrich Schroeder announced the men's sentences, he accused Gruna & Jahr, *Stern*'s publishers, of being so eager to print the volumes, and thereby boost both the magazine's circulation and their own income, that they did not examine the volumes to verify their authenticity before publishing them. The judge charged the magazine with a "grotesque performance" in buying the diaries and publishing excerpts from them. "No one [at *Stern*] asked, 'Are the diaries really valid?' " Judge Schroeder admonished the publishers. Citing examples of the errors that abounded in the volumes, the judge found the listing of seventy-eight generals who were promoted by Hitler, exasperating, "Who would ever write down the names of seventy-eight generals in a diary?"

Stern made a public statement accepting the court's ruling: "*Stern* regrets that it has brought journalism into discredit."

While Gerd Heidemann and Konrad Kujau languished in prison, the West German magazine suffered its own agony. The circulation figures dropped as a result of the publication of the bogus diaries and have yet to stop falling.

The Hitler diaries forgery, if not the world's greatest hoax, was, however, due to its many flaws, one of the most quickly unmasked. As someone at *Stern* declared, "The biggest post-war journalistic scoop has become the biggest journalistic mistake of all time." The Hitler diaries, touted as the Find of the Century, turned out to be the Fake of the Year.

CHAPTER THREE

FAKE DOCUMENTS & LETTERS

How can a forgery such as the Hitler diaries, which was riddled with mistakes, fool experts? Clifford Irving, the forger of entrepreneur Howard Hughes' autobiography, says forging sixty-two volumes of Hitler's handwriting "would be entirely possible for someone intelligent, gifted, and artistic. Once you have the mood, you can go on forever."

Judges who preside at forgery trials disagree. They claim that a person's signature counts as much as fingerprints in weighing evidence. Handwriting experts side with the judges, insisting experts rarely make mistakes when examining a suspected forged document. Many document detectives point out that there are no better tools for studying handwriting than good eyes and a microscope. Comparing two documents placed side by side under a microscope has changed so little over the years that analysts still refer to Albert Osborn's textbook on the subject, which was written in 1929.

Osborn claimed, "A man's writing seems to be a part of his very flesh and bones; he cannot discard it at will." Osborn insisted that people added unconscious habits when writing, such as the way they crossed "t's," dotted "i's," or how high they wrote capital and small letters. It is impossible to eliminate all of these habits when copying another person's handwriting, or to incorporate all the handwriting quirks of another person into a forged document. Osborn noted, "Any time you try to change your writing, you do things that look unnatural."

Chief of the FBI's document laboratory Gary Herbertson concurs, saying, "A forger's writing doesn't have the speed . . . or smoothness of natural writing. You can see blunt beginnings and ends of strokes . . . inappropriate breaks (in letters) . . . you can tell if one's written quickly and the other is carefully drawn . . ."

According to experts, the best way to prevent forgery is to make documents hard to copy. They point out that Hitler's undistinguished scrawl was relatively easy to forge, and thus could fool some experts. Given that fact, says writer John Tierney, "It's safe to assume . . . that the John Hancock diaries won't hit the newsstands soon."

An advantage for handwriting detectives today is that most people's writing is hasty and somewhat sloppy, compared to the careful, uniform script once taught in schools. This means that each person's handwriting is more individualistic, which makes it harder for the forger to copy and easier for investigators to detect genuine works from frauds.

Testing of paper is another way analysts detect forgeries. Handwriting authority Mary Benjamin notes that parchment was used until about 1150, when rag paper, made by stretching paper across wires that left visible lines on it, became popular. After 1800, woven paper, in which fibers can be seen, was used. By 1860, wood-pulp paper became commonplace. Many forgers have been caught because they used the wrong kind of paper for their document.

Experts also examine a paper's watermarks. These are distinguishing designs embedded in the paper during its manufacture and can be seen by holding the paper up to a light. Each manufacturer uses different watermarks, each of which is catalogued and thus traceable.

The type of ink used helps to verify old documents as well. For example, ink made of ground carbon was used until 1020. This does not tint and wear through the paper with age. Iron-gall ink, used until around 1860, does show wear however and aniline ink, used after 1860, disappears when submerged in water. One collector of rare autographs proved a valuable document was genuine, wholly by accident. A hurricane blew his paper into water where it remained for five days. When the man found the paper, he sighed with relief, as all the signatures remained clear. His document had been written with iron-gall ink.

Other times the type of pen used to write a document gives away whether the work is a forgery. The quill pen was used exclusively until around 1780, when the steel pen came into vogue. Fiber-tipped pens were not used extensively in the United States until 1964. The different marks each pen makes can be detected under a microscope.

To detect forgeries more quickly, modern researchers are trying to establish a standard formula based upon measurements of angles and heights of letters. Other researchers are experimenting with computers, which would verify signatures by measuring the spaces between letters, the angle at which the pen was held, and the pressure put on the pen. At West Germany's Mannheim University, researchers are developing an electric grid microscope to measure precisely the indentations made by pens. Also, a pen can be attached to a computer, which will direct the pen to retrace a writing sample. The computer then analyzes sixteen writing tendencies. Recently, five thousand forged signatures were fed into a computer, and the microchip detective let only one forgery go by undetected.

The Mussolini Diaries

> For the love of God, Panvini, hide them in a safe place.

According to Amalia Panvini, this order was issued to her father by Benito Mussolini's minister as he entrusted Panvini with an important package. Like Hitler, the Italian dictator was also worried about the victorious Allies obtaining his documents and personal papers. If Mussolini were tried for committing war crimes, these documents could provide the proof to convict him.

In 1957, Amalia Panvini, then forty-three, and her mother, Rosa, then seventy-five, claimed they possessed these previously hidden, handwritten, Benito Mussolini diaries. Amalia offered to sell the diaries to *Life* magazine and to the Italian newspaper *Corriere della Sera*. Amalia contended that she needed money to support herself and her mother.

Vittorio Mussolini, the dictator's son, examined the handwriting in the alleged diaries and concluded the writing was his father's. An expert handwriting analyst conducted chemical tests comparing the diaries with Mussolini's genuine handwriting and agreed, saying, "Thirty volumes of manuscript cannot be the work of a forger, but of a genius. You can falsify a few lines or even pages, but not a series of diaries."

As occurred in the Hitler forgery, the many volumes composing the Mussolini diaries added weight to their authenticity. Handwriting expert Charles Hamilton says some forgers copy long works of famous people for that very reason. In addition, Hamilton said, "The [Mussolini] journals were accompanied by forged bills of lading, receipts . . . the way the Hitler diaries also came with a lot of corroborating material. It's a technique forgers frequently use." However, adds Hamilton, this corroborating material often becomes the forgers' undoing. Forgers frequently make the mistake of painstakingly copying the valued signature or document, then carelessly forging the handwriting of secondary signatures or material connected to the document, such as secretaries' memos, invoices, and receipts. Expert Kenneth Rendell notes that many excellent Benjamin Franklin forgeries include a hastily scrawled receipt, allegedly signed by then Pennsylvania treasurer David Rittenhouse.

Lending further credence to the authenticity of the Mussolini diaries was the fact they were written in school exercise books like those the dictator used. They also included many of Mussolini's private thoughts, such as "Hitler is mad! Our ideas are diametrically opposed."

Fortunately, before any publication purchased the diaries, Vittorio Mussolini examined them again and found many historical and linguistic faults, which made him conclude the diaries were fakes. The Italian police raided the Panvini home and confiscated all but four of the volumes. Police charged the Panvini women with forgery and fraud. Rosa admitted she spent years perfecting Mussolini's handwriting to produce the diaries. Both women were given suspended sentences.

In 1968, the London *Sunday Times* bought the remaining four volumes from the Panvinis for seventy-one thousand dollars. As human interest stories from Italy were not the most popular international articles of the day, the *Sunday Times* was unaware of the women's arrest. When the *Times* learned of the hoax, they cancelled publication. Shortly thereafter, Rosa Panvini died.

In 1983, the Mussolini diaries resurfaced when Amalia Panvini said her fifteen-year-old confession was a hoax. She claimed she had confessed to the Mussolini forgery in order to avoid being sent to prison. Amalia insisted that neither she nor her mother had forged the diaries. When asked who had, she answered, "Who knows?"

The Lincoln Love Letters—The Minor Affair

At last, after nearly a century, appear the priceless documents which lift the veil shrouding the love affair between Abraham Lincoln and young Ann Rutledge.

This claim appeared in the December, 1928, issue of the *Atlantic Monthly* magazine as an introduction to a forthcoming series entitled "Lincoln The Lover." For years Americans had speculated upon the rumor that Ann Rutledge was Abraham Lincoln's first and only true love.

The person who lifted the veil off the rumor was Miss Wilma Frances Minor, a former actress turned newspaper columnist for the San Diego, California, *Union*. She claimed the collection had been passed down through her mother's (Mrs. Cora De-Boyer) side of the family and offered to sell the letters to the editor of *Atlantic Monthly*, Ellery Sedgwick.

In addition to romantic soliloquies between Ann and Lincoln when they were in their twenties, the so-called Lincoln love letters included diary pages of Matilda ("Mat") Cameron, Ann's cousin and best friend; letters from Lincoln to John Calhoun, a Democratic politician and Lincoln's benefactor; a memorandum about Lincoln written by John Calhoun's daughter Sally; and four books signed and annotated by Lincoln.

Sedgwick, hoping to use the series for an *Atlantic Monthly* Christmas subscription promotion, wanted to print the letters as soon as possible. He offered Miss Minor a one-thousand-dollar advance, plus four thousand on publication.

Sedgwick also asked famous Lincoln scholar Reverend William E. Barton, who had spent his life trying to unmask the many legends surrounding Abraham Lincoln, to examine the collection. Barton reported to Sedgwick that the letters contained too many references to historical data for love letters and the sentiments expressed were too consistent with the rumored love-tragedy to be genuine. For example, one letter, supposedly written by Lincoln shortly after Ann died from malaria in 1835, stated: "Like a ray of sunshine and as brief—she flooded my life, and at times like today when I traverse past paths I see this picture before me—fever burning the light from her dear eyes, urging me to fight for the right."

When Reverend Barton met Miss Minor in person, however, he was so swept away by her charm that he reversed his verdict. He told Sedgwick he had misgivings about the love letters' authenticity but held out hope they would be proved genuine. Barton's previous misgivings went unquestioned since other experts also believed in the letters' authenticity. The poet Carl Sandburg, Lincoln's most famous biographer, said, "These new letters seem entirely authentic—preciously and wonderfully coordinate and chime with all else known of Lincoln."

Historian Paul M. Angle, then the executive secretary of the Abraham Lincoln Association, tested the letters and found the ink, paper, handwriting, content, and historical facts filled with errors. When the *Atlantic Monthly* printed the first article, most critics disagreed with Sandburg and did not believe the letters were genuine. The editor of the Massachusetts Historical Society wrote Sedgwick: "You are putting over one of the crudest forgeries I have known."

Historians pointed out the letters were signed "Abe" although it was well known that Lincoln detested that nickname. Experts took exception to Lincoln's alleged choice of words in writing "Mary is well, thank the Lord . . ." when Lincoln always spoke of "God" unless he was quoting. In addition, no references were found that mentioned John Calhoun's ever having a daughter named Sally.

Perhaps the most glaring error was a May 9, 1834, letter to John Calhoun, in which Lincoln said, "The Bixby's are leaving this week for some place in Kansas." The area called Kansas today was not organized into a territory until 1854. In the same letter, Lincoln referred to a land tract as "Section 40" at a time in history when townships were divided into only thirty-six sections. Historians emphasized that Lincoln was a land surveyor, and would never have made such an error.

Even Ellery Sedgwick was bewildered by a letter supposedly from Ann to Abraham in which she spoke of practicing handwriting using Spencer's copybook. Spencer's first book on penmanship was not published until thirteen years after Ann's death.

Critical editorials about the love letters appeared in newspapers across the United States. A *New York Times* writer stated that the country should be relieved if the Lincoln letters were forgeries since, if authentic, they would leave an image of a "slobbering, inflated, illiterate Lincoln."

Eventually Carl Sandburg reversed his "authentic" vote, as did Reverend Barton, who wrote to Wilma Minor: "I have come to the conviction that the letters which you are sending to the *Atlantic* . . . are not genuine. And, my dear, I am afraid you know it."

The magazine's circulation manager wrote Wilma suggesting she initiate a lawsuit against Barton. Miss Minor's mother wrote back that her daughter could not face such an ordeal. The magazine staff was ecstatic—but not about Mrs. DeBoyer's reply. Scrutinizing her letter, they realized the handwriting was identical to that in the Lincoln Love Letters.

Pressured by the dissenting chorus of Lincoln experts, Ellery Sedgwick hired private detectives to investigate Miss Minor. The investigators compounded the evidence for forgery by learning from James Ashe, head of a publishing company in San Diego, that Miss Minor frequently arranged interviews at Ashe's office with his authors, supposedly for her newspaper column. When she interviewed Scott Greene, son of a friend of Lincoln's, she told Ashe that Greene had letters signed by Lincoln and Ann Rutledge that she hoped to buy. Ashe confessed to being surprised when the articles appeared written by Miss Minor without any reference to Scott Greene.

When the hoax was exposed, Wilma Minor and her mother were charged with fraud. Miss Minor signed a confession saying her mother had composed the letters through messages given her by spirits: "The spirits of Ann and Abe were speaking through my mother to me so that my gifts as a writer combined with her gifts as a medium could hand in something worthwhile to the world."

Ellery Sedgwick issued a statement withdrawing the articles from publication. Neither Frances Wilma Minor nor her mother was ever prosecuted. The world will therefore have to wait until someone rummages through a great-great-great relative's basement and, shoved into a dusty corner inside a weather-worn box of mementos, finds the true story of "Lincoln The Lover."

The Protocols of The Elders of Zion

Of the thousands of false documents created over the centuries, one has had a particularly lasting and degrading effect upon a group of people. The people are Jews, and the hoax is the Protocols of The Elders of Zion. Supposedly the minutes from the first Zionist Congress held in Basel, Switzerland, in 1897, the Protocols may well be called the most odious forgery ever committed.

Perpetrators of the deception claimed that a group of Jews, the Learned Elders, had met to plan a Jewish takeover of the world. The twenty-four Protocols detailed the methods the Jews were supposedly planning, including, "to overthrow Christian civilization, corrupt the younger generation by subversive education, amuse people to prevent them from thinking, ferment international hatreds, destroy family life, undermine respect for religion, weaken human bodies by inoculation with microbes, and prepare for universal bankruptcy and concentration of gold in the hands of the Jews."

The Protocols first appeared in Russia in a St. Petersburg newspaper in 1903. At that time, the perpetrators' motive was apparently to suppress and discredit radical and progressive groups in Russia by making them appear dupes of the Jews. The Russian Secret Police of Czar Nicholas II are presumed to be the instigators of the hoax, yet the identity of the original forger has never been discovered. In 1921, a reporter for the London *Times* found two sources from which the Protocols had been copied. The allegation of Jewish leaders plotting secretly came from a novel published in 1868 entitled *Biarritz*, by Hermann Goedsche. Goedsche was German but used the pseudonym Sir John Retcliffe. The language and ideas in the alleged Protocols, however, were stolen directly from a French satire published in 1864 entitled, *Dialogue aux Enfers entre Montesquieu et Machiavelli, (Dialogue in Hell Between Montesquieu and Machiavelli)*, which discusses the powers of corruption and how to attain them. The forgers of the Protocols adapted Machiavelli's thoughts to fit their fictitious Elders.

Czar Nicholas refused to authorize the use of the Protocols for his own purposes once he learned they were forged. However, the perpetrators circulated the false document secretly throughout Russia. Today the Protocols of The Elders of Zion is still a potent weapon for anti-Jewish violence and is espoused by organized hate groups such as the Ku Klux Klan and the neo-Nazis. British historian Christopher Sykes has called the Protocols "one of the biggest lies ever devised by a liar, and for that reason there will for long be fools to believe it."

Although the Protocols have been proved a hoax many times, the forged document continues to be translated into many languages and published in countries the world over. The intention of those who still perpetrate the hoax today remains the same as that of its originators in Czarist Russia—the justification for hatred of Jews.

The Alfred Dreyfus Affair

In the latter part of the nineteenth century, anti-semitism in France was particularly virulent. In 1894, some officers in the French army forged papers proving that another officer, Captain Alfred Dreyfus, a Jew, had passed secret information to the Germans and Italians. Dreyfus was convicted of treason and sentenced to life imprisonment on Devils' Island. The captain's sentence included a degrading public ceremony in which his sword was broken and his insignia ripped off his uniform.

The French novelist Emile Zola believed in Dreyfus' innocence and wrote a book entitled *J'Accuse*. The book resulted in his own two-year prison sentence, which was later reversed on appeal. Due to public sentiment against him, Zola left France to live in England.

French officer, Alfred Dreyfus, who was the victim of a faked letter implicating him as a spy.

Believers in Dreyfus persisted in proving his innocence, and four years after his first conviction discovered that Colonel Henry, head of French Intelligence, had forged the documents. When exposed, Colonel Henry committed suicide rather than face public disgrace. Historians are convinced a Major Esterhazy was the originator of the plan to incriminate Dreyfus. However, Esterhazy was tried and acquitted.

Finally, in 1899, eleven years and two trials later, Dreyfus was tried again and found innocent. His former conviction was deleted from criminal records, and he was restored to his full military rank. When Emile Zola died in 1902, he was no longer blamed for defending Dreyfus and was given a state funeral in France. Captain Alfred Dreyfus was awarded the French Legion of Honor.

Joseph Cosey, Master Forger

One day in 1929, a forty-two-year-old man entered the Library of Congress in Washington, D.C., and headed for the Original Manuscripts Room. After reviewing a large box of historical letters, memos, and government papers, the man, born Martin Coneely, felt his love of eighteenth and nineteenth-century Americana surface. Carefully, he slipped one of the papers into his pocket. On the way out, he obliged the guard by signing the visitors' register Joseph Cosey, his favorite of six aliases.

Since the Library of Congress did not check the contents of the box before returning it to the stacks, the historical paper is still unofficially missing from the Library's collection. The stolen memorandum served as the catalyst by which Joseph Cosey earned a national reputation as a forger of historical documents. Professionals call this type of forgery *archeological forgery*. The document Cosey stole was a 1786 pay warrant signed by Benjamin Franklin when he was president of the Supreme Executive Council of Pennsylvania.

Joseph Cosey might never have become "the most skillful autograph forger of this century," as Charles Hamilton calls him, if he had not been broke about a year later and tried to sell the Franklin signature. When an autograph dealer called the memorandum a fake, Cosey was so outraged that he swore to return with a forged signature and convince the dealer it was genuine.

After months spent in libraries copying signatures of famous men in American history, Cosey discovered he could reproduce Abraham Lincoln's handwriting the best. Thus he signed "Yours truly, A. Lincoln" on a scrap of paper and submitted it to the dealer, who bought the "authentic signature" for ten dollars.

Encouraged by his success, Cosey spent from the beginning of the 1930s until the end of World War II flooding the country with his forged signatures, including those of authors Edgar Allan Poe, Walt Whitman, Mark Twain, and Rudyard Kipling, evangelist Mary Baker Eddy, and political figures Alexander Hamilton, Thomas Jefferson, George Washington, John and Sam Adams, and Patrick Henry. Cosey became so proficient at forging signatures that he began inventing forged texts to go with the signatures. These Cosey texts, until found to be forgeries, became "newly discovered" American history.

Experts say that except for the crime of forgery, Joseph Cosey stayed within the law. He never claimed his forgeries were genuine, but instead would invent a story about how he had acquired the document, then leave the decision as to its authenticity up to the dealer. Other times he would offer his documents for appraisal only, knowing that if the dealer thought a manuscript genuine, he would probably offer to buy it.

In addition, Cosey never sold his forgeries to amateur collectors. "I take pleasure in fooling the professionals," he said. The professionals stung by Cosey's artistic hand included some of the nation's most distinguished autograph dealers and auction houses. The Parke-Bernet Galleries, considered America's most prestigious auction house, once scheduled a Cosey-forged

Lincoln document for sale. The Gallery appraised the document at fifteen hundred dollars. The document was discovered to be a fake before anyone made a bid.

The New York Public Library bestowed an unusual honor upon Joseph Cosey in 1934. When the library tried to remove Cosey's forgeries from circulation, a special file, known as the Cosey Collection, was set up. Additional Cosey forgeries continue to be added. In 1934 that file, if genuine, would have been worth one hundred thousand dollars.

Even though he forged documents so prolifically, Joseph Cosey was only caught once. He was finally identified when he forged a document signed by Benjamin Franklin in 1757 and presented it to an autograph dealer as dated 1787, when Franklin's signature is known to have betrayed his old age by its crabbed, shaky strokes.

Cosey's trail vanished in 1954. Although he is presumed to have died by now, his forgeries continue to appear at auctions, antique shops, and second-hand bookstores. Joseph Cosey has earned the ultimate distinction of the archeological forger— even when his works are known to be bogus, people want to buy them. At three to five dollars per forgery, the price is even affordable.

Today some handwriting experts believe that as computerized technology becomes more accessible, hardly anyone will write by hand anymore. Therefore, handwritten signatures will become harder to find, and eventually the forger's art could become obsolete. Other experts disagree, saying that as long as there are famous books, poems, letters, and plays written by celebrated individuals, the forger's pen will never run dry.

The Man Who Owned Arizona

One of the most audacious deceptions involved a treaty between the United States and Mexico, called the Gadsen Purchase. Passed in 1853, the treaty added southern Arizona

James Addison Reavis, alias Don Miguel de Peralta or The Baron of Arizona.

and part of New Mexico to territories of the United States. However, the government would still honor pretreaty titles to land in these territories if the claimant held a land grant signed by King Ferdinand VI of Spain.

Enter James Addison Reavis. While a soldier in the Civil War, Reavis developed his talent for forgery by faking the signatures of commanding officers on leave passes and then selling the forged passes to other soldiers. After the war, Reavis traveled to Santa Fe, New Mexico, where he learned about the Spanish land grants. He immediately switched from petty forgery to hoaxing on a grand scale, the results of which have never been experienced since.

First he invented a fictitious identity, a Spanish nobleman named Don Miguel de Peralta, plus several generations of Peralta's Spanish family. To provide genealogical evidence of his fictitious family, Reavis traveled to cities throughout the American Southwest, Mexico, and Spain, where he sneaked phony documents into public archives. Next he forged a land grant made out to Peralta, signed by the King of Spain, for seventeen thousand square miles of Arizona's prime land, including Phoenix, the state capital, and land bearing Arizona's major gold, silver, and copper mines. Reavis then presented the grant to government authorities in 1881.

Reavis' land claim exploded into a controversy that shook the entire nation. Years passed while lawyers contested his claim. In the meantime, the ugly part of the hoax was that thousands of Americans already lived and worked on this land. Until, and if, Reavis' claim was declared invalid, these people faced unemployment and housing problems if they did not pay rent to Reavis. Reavis also offered to rent his land to the industries and homesteaders "trespassing" on his property. Thus he became the landlord of the Southern Pacific Railroad and the company paid him fifty thousand dollars, a fortune in the 1880s, for the right to run their railroad across his land. At the same time, Reavis offered to sell his grant to the government for fifty million dollars.

In 1893, the U.S. Court of Private Land Grant Claims hired a special investigator, who found some of Reavis' land grant documents had been written on parchment produced after the time of King Ferdinand. In addition, the investigator discovered the claims were written in two types of ink, and contained many historical errors.

Reavis was arrested in 1895, and put in prison. The one-time millionaire hoaxer, died in jail a pauper. Foolishly confident that the Claim Court would declare his land grant valid, and he would become the rightful owner of the state of Arizona, James Addison Reavis had spent every penny of his "rent money."

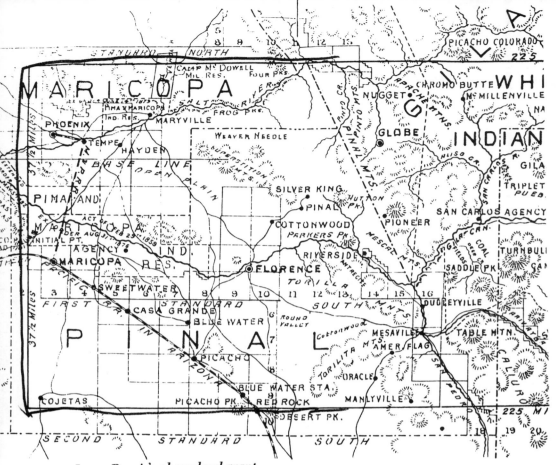

James Reavis's phony land grant.

Historical Hoaxes

Historical facts have been repeatedly victims of the forger's pen. Some forgers invent their own versions of history. The danger here lies in the fact that false historical accounts distort the continuing montage of world history, as many generations of readers may be affected by a book's fake contents.

For example, an English professor once forged a history book of fourth-century Britain. The professor also created a fictitious map of the area which contained at least one hundred nonexistent towns, roads, and other sites. His history was considered

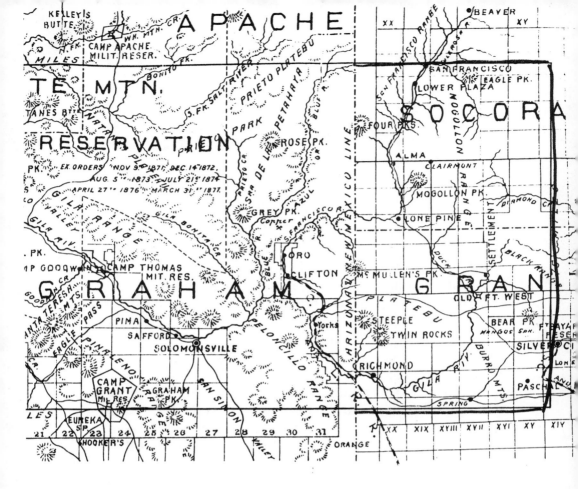

an important reference source, and the English author Edward Gibbon acknowledged the book in his classic history, *The Decline and Fall of the Roman Empire*. Not until one hundred years later was the work discovered to be a fake. By that time however, the false historical accounts and map sites had been printed in so many other reference books that historians claimed that finding all the other affected books and deleting the wrong information was an impossible task.

Several myths revolve around the renowned naval hero John Paul Jones. For years, the chief biography of Jones was *Life of*

John Paul Jones, by Augustus C. Buell. In 1906, a Mrs. Reginald de Koven examined the biography and found it to be "the most audacious historical forgery ever put out upon a credulous public." References listed in Buell's bibliography were nonexistent, including their authors.

A glaring error in the book dealt with John Paul adding Jones to his name. Buell stated John did so to please a William Jones, who promised in return to remember John in his will. However, William Jones never left John Paul a penny; John never qualified as Jones' heir; and John Paul Jones never inherited anything from anyone in his life.

A fantastic sequel to the Buell fake biography was one written by Alfred Henry Lewis. When Lewis was congratulated on having written the only authentic life of Jones, Lewis replied: "That's [the Buell biography] the only book about Paul Jones I ever read. I just took it and translated it into my own language. If it's all wrong, so's my book."

In the early nineteenth century, traditional autobiographies were called memoirs and were intimate accounts of a person's life. In America, men and women wrote their own memoirs, while Europeans often employed ghostwriters to do the work for them. These unheralded authors frequently moonlighted by writing their own version of a person's life history, without the person's knowledge or consent.

The Emperor Napoleon did not escape the fake biographer either. Historical expert Augustine Thierry states that a majority of the Napoleonic memoirs published between 1825 and 1840 were forgeries. One forger, De Lamothe-Langon, alias Etienne Leon, was said to have run a factory to produce fake memoirs including those of Marie Antoinette, the Duchesse de Berry, Cardinal Richelieu, and Frederick the Great, among others.

For many years after the guillotine was invented, a story circulated that the first man to be executed by the device was its so-called inventor, Dr. Guillotin. On May 28, 1738, the two hundredth anniversary of Dr. Guillotin's birth, a reporter for the London *Daily Telegraph* wrote that the good doctor did not die by its blade. His legal death certificate, found in France's Cluny Museum, stated that Dr. Guillotin died a natural death a few days before his one hundredth birthday. According to the *Telegraph*'s reporter, Guillotin did not even invent the beheading device. Known as the "manaia," the guillotine had existed in Italy for centuries before its alleged invention in France during the French Revolution. Dr. Guillotin's contribution to history was merely to suggest a humane way of carrying out death sentences in France.

Not only has Abraham Lincoln's signature been forged more than anyone else's, but his faked signature has been used to create equally false myths about him. One reason Dr. Barton wrote *The Life of Abraham Lincoln* was that "all the extant biographies of Lincoln contain inaccuracies, some of them trivial, others important, and few of them grave." Author Lloyd D. Lewis claimed in his book *Myths After Lincoln* that the reason so many immortalizing legends were created about the nation's sixteenth President was that Americans wanted to give the country a hero to worship. One of the most popular legends, still found in American history books, is called the Bixby Letter, named after the mother to whom President Lincoln supposedly wrote expressing his sorrow that her five sons were killed fighting for the Union during the Civil War. Reverend Barton exposed the myth by finding proof that not all Mrs. Bixby's sons enlisted in the army, and not all who did were killed.

Another Lincoln fable has the President showing up a day late for his wedding to Mary Todd. Yet another myth claims Lincoln dreamed he was going to die and told his cabinet about his dream on the day of his assassination.

Not content merely to keep Abraham Lincoln on a mythological pedestal, the legend makers have also invented tales about Lincoln's assassin, John Wilkes Booth. Even today these fabrications are readily accepted as true, since the events surrounding Lincoln's assassination are sketchy. The documented facts that Booth easily entered the President's box at Ford Theater and escaped unimpeded have resulted in speculation that a conspiracy was behind the assassination. When Booth was later shot and killed, Secretary of State Seward demanded absolute secrecy in disposing of Booth's body, which resulted in the persistent myth that the person killed for Lincoln's murder was not John Wilkes Booth. But who *was* shot for Lincoln's murder? To this day, no one can say for sure.

CHAPTER FOUR

LITERARY HOAXES

In the Huntington Library in San Marino, California, fifty-four first-edition books from the Victorian school of writers occupy a prominent position on the shelves. Almost every British author from the last half of the nineteenth century is represented in these first editions, including Rudyard Kipling, George Eliot, Robert Louis Stevenson, Alfred Lord Tennyson, Charles Dickens, and Elizabeth Barrett Browning, whose collection *Sonnets from the Portuguese* is one of the most notable.

Except for one flaw, the books would sell for a king's ransom at any auction. Even so the library is extremely proud to own these flawed first editions, since it means the Huntington Library houses the largest single collection of literary forgeries in the world. Many of these were created when forgers excerpted long poems from already published works and then republished them as pamphlets under an earlier date.

Forging literature written by scholarly or famous people is another way hoaxers make fortunes—and headlines. Compared

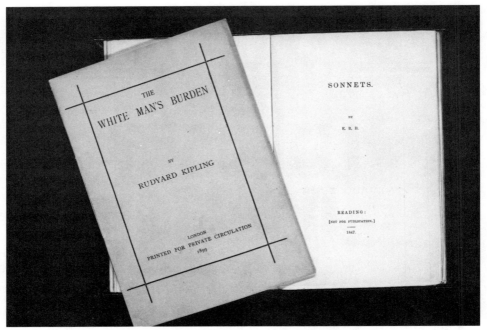

Forged first editions of books by Rudyard Kipling and Elizabeth Barrett Browning.

to faking a signature or a document, literary forgery requires learning both the handwriting of the person being imitated and the person's literary style. Since the first symbol was etched into stone, the written word has garnered a special respect for its author. For literary hoaxers, seeing their book, play, or other written material in print is a giant ego boost. And, their excitement is increased by imagining others reading the words inside the book. All writers feel that a certain immortality will be theirs through the lasting existence of their books. Literary forgers are no exception. The prospect of immortality is frequently just as important to the forger as becoming famous and wealthy.

For centuries, literary scholars have had to sort out plagiarism, thefts, and dishonest handling of material from an author's original works. Most beginning writers study the works of great authors and often try to copy their style. Copying another writer's style is an effective learning technique and can help a writer to learn to recognize his or her own voice. If that writer then claims his or her own work to be that of the master however, then the writer has crossed the line to forgery.

Sometimes writers, doubtful of their ability to succeed on their own, invent mythical authors for their literary works until they have gained substantial fame. During the 1760s, an English boy named Thomas Chatterton, fearing critics would not take the writing of a teenager seriously, invented a fifteenth-century monk named Thomas Rowley and wrote medieval romantic poetry under the monk's name. Chatterton claimed he found the poems in the treasure room of the church where his uncle was a deacon. Other poets doubted the existence of the monk Rowley, and Chatterton was soon discovered to be the true author and proclaimed a fraud. Thomas was young and destitute, and when his hoax was unmasked, he felt even more like a failure. Thomas Chatterton climbed the stairs to his attic room and committed suicide by drinking arsenic.

Part of the tragedy was that if Chatterton had trusted his own ability, he most likely would have been a success in his own right. His Rowley poems were published posthumously and received critical merit. Famous English authors such as Byron, Shelley, Coleridge, Southey, and Wordsworth claimed Thomas Chatterton was a genius and praised the originality, imagery, and lyrical beauty of his poems. Chatterton's style was compared to the English poet Keats, who admired Chatterton so much that he dedicated his epic poem *Endymion* to Chatterton's memory.

Occasionally, writers invent fictitious authors of their works *after* they have gained fame and recognition. One such author was French novelist Romain Gary. To get revenge on the Paris literary establishment, who he thought had undervalued his talent and written him off prematurely, Gary wrote four novels using the invented name of Emile Ajar. One of these novels, *La*

Vie Devant Soi (*His Whole Life Ahead of Him*), won the French Goncourat Award, which Gary had previously won under his own name for his novel *The Roots of Heaven*. The fictitious Emile Ajar's novel was made into an Academy Award-winning film titled *Madame Rosa*.

Romain Gary initiated rumors that Emile Ajar was in fact his second cousin Paul Pavlowitch and corresponded with the press using addresses in Brazil, Denmark, and Switzerland. Since his American publisher had never seen him in person, Gary granted interviews in which he posed as Pavlowitch, although he always insisted these meetings be held outside of France, where he would not be recognized.

Others speculated that Ajar was Gary, but at least two critics claimed Gary did not have the writing talent to produce such good novels. Other critics speculated that Ajar used the help of a collaborator, most likely Romain Gary.

The novels Romain Gary wrote under Emile Ajar's name have an underlying theme of loneliness, age, and despair. Given this fact, the way Gary's hoax was revealed becomes less surprising. Gary himself unmasked his deception in "Life and Death of Emile Ajar," which was an appended essay to his last novel, entitled *King Solomon*.

His essay said that if he could have arranged it, he would have continued writing forever, without submitting anything for publication, so that the Paris literary critics he so disdained would have to belittle other authors. His appended essay was released posthumously, as Gary had planned, for on December 2, 1983, Gary committed suicide. In his own way, Romain Gary seems to have had the last laugh on his critics, as he wrote in his suicide essay: "I've had a lot of fun. Goodbye, and thank you."

In contrast to the tragic motivation of Romain Gary's literary hoax, British author Doris Lessing's reasons for inventing a fictitious author for two of her novels are on a lighter side.

Wanting to prove her theory that new writers do not get the attention from publishers they deserve, she wrote a novel entitled *The Diary of a Good Neighbor* and a sequel entitled *If Only the Old Could* . . . under the name of Jane Somers. She submitted the *Diary* novel first. Two British publishers rejected it out of hand as "too depressing." A third publisher bought the book, commenting that it bore a resemblance to Doris Lessing. Only Lessing's American editor, Robert Gottlieb, Editor-in-Chief of Alfred Knopf, recognized immediately that Lessing was the novel's true author. "As soon as I read it, I burst into laughter," Gottlieb said, "because it was a voice that is so well known to me." He swore to remain silent while Doris played out her deception.

Lessing also wanted to get back at critics who had pigeon-holed her first as a feminist writer, then later as an author of visionary science fiction. As she said, "I wanted to be reviewed on merit, as a new writer, without the benefit of a 'name,' to get free of that cage of associations and labels that every established writer has to learn to live inside."

Doris Lessing proved her point. With no famous author to promote, Jane Somers received a handful of reviews and sales of under three thousand copies. In comparison, Lessing's hardcover novels usually sell between fifteen and thirty thousand copies. "It was interesting to be a beginning writer again," Lessing said. "You are patted on the head and found promising."

When rumors started to leak about Jane Somers' true identity, Lessing unmasked her own hoax. "The single most astonishing fact is that nobody guessed it was me," she said, then added, "A very good first novel can get published and get good reviews and then vanish. Few publishers have the attitude they used to have: keep the writers in print."

The two Somer novels were reissued in one paperback volume titled *The Diaries of Jane Somers*, with an introduction by Doris Lessing describing the hoax. Sales expectations were on the high side. Lessing claimed the irony of the hoax was that if she had not revealed the deception, "poor old Jane Somers could have faded away forever."

The William Shakespeare Forgeries

> When you have eliminated the impossible, whatever remains,
> however improbable, must be the truth.
>
> Sir Arthur Conan Doyle
> *Sherlock Holmes, The Sign of Fear* (1890)

Most hoaxers would agree with Mr. Doyle, as improbability
has never been their concern. In the eighteenth century,
William Henry Ireland, seventeen-year-old son of Samuel Ireland, a noted painter and engraver, decided he could change his
father's low opinion of him into one of tremendous pride by
granting his father's most ardent wish—to own an authentic
Shakespeare letter. William Henry merely forged one—a property deed to land near the Old Globe Theater, where Shakespeare's plays were produced.

Ireland cut a piece of parchment from an old document, then
persuaded a bookbinder to make him a bottle of ink that would
look dark and aged on the parchment. Ireland's father was so
ecstatic with the "authentic" Shakespeare deed that William
Henry, eager to further increase his father's opinion of him,
forged more Shakespeare material, including a love poem to
Shakespeare's wife Ann Hathaway, books from Shakespeare's
own library with marginal notes supposedly written by the
bard, and a thank-you note from Queen Elizabeth. Ireland
became so carried away with his hoax that he even "found" a box
containing some locks of Shakespeare's hair. Then, he presented the forgeries to his father, who gave William Henry the
fatherly praise he craved.

When Ireland forged the original manuscript of *King Lear*
and portions of *Hamlet* he altered Shakespeare's text, changing
lines and cutting out some of the comedy. He also flattened the
verse by exchanging Shakespeare's metaphors and imagery for
his own direct statements. One critic commented that these
newly discovered texts showed Shakespeare's "straight, manly
style."

William told his father that he had obtained the manuscripts and other documents from a man he had met in a coffee shop who, when he learned of William's avid interest in Shakespeare, invited him to look through an antique chest in his house that was filled with old documents and papers. The stranger said he could have anything he wanted so long as he kept the gentleman's identity a secret. William called him "Mr. H."

Samuel begged William to look for more Shakespeare treasures at Mr. H's house. William, ever eager to be loved and respected in his father's eyes, forged a "Profession of Faith," which he said was signed by Shakespeare shortly before his death and which declared the bard's allegiance to Protestantism. This document pleased not only William Henry's father, but the Church of England as well, since it thus discounted rumors that Shakespeare was influenced by the Papacy, which was in disfavor in England during Shakespeare's day. The "Profession of Faith" was examined by an expert and pronounced genuine. Samuel Ireland became famous, as celebrities traveled to his painting and engraving shop to view the original Shakespeare documents and manuscripts.

William Henry's ego reached a peak, and he embarked upon his most daring forgery yet. He wrote a complete, five-act Shakespeare play, which he named *Vortigern and Rowena* after a painting of the Anglo-Saxon king that hung in the Ireland's living room. Much later, when writing his confession, William Henry noted, "It is extraordinary to observe how willingly persons will blind themselves on any point interesting to their feelings. When it was known that a play on the subject of Vortigern was coming forward, every person who inspected the manuscript admired the strange coincidence of Mr. Ireland's having so long possessed a drawing on the very subject of the drama. Yet . . . not even in one instance did the drawing . . . excite the slightest suspicion."

Ireland copied the play from *Hollingshead's Chronicles*, the source book for many of Shakespeare's plots. *Vortigern and Rowena*, suspiciously similar to Shakespeare's *Macbeth*, is about an ambitious nobleman who murders his way to the throne. The play was actually produced at the Drury Lane Theatre in London. Richard Sheridan, a playwright, and at the time owner of the Drury Lane, read a few scenes and commented, "There are certainly some bold ideas, but they are crude and undigested. . . . One would be led to believe that Shakespeare must have been very young when he wrote the play."

Sheridan assigned the actor John Kimble to produce *Vortigern* as well as to play the title role. Kimble was one of the growing number of skeptics who believed that William Henry had forged the never-before-produced Shakespeare play. Kimble tried to sabotage *Vortigern* on opening night by making the production look ridiculous. He assigned a terrible actor with a squeaky voice to portray one of the parts. The man's appearance was deemed so funny that the audience burst into gales of laughter every time the actor opened his mouth. Kimble put uncalled-for stress on the line "And when this solemn mockery is ended" that sent the audience into more howls of ridicule. During the play, doubters and believers in the work's authenticity started a shouting match that eventually broke out into a fight. After the final, crucial death scene, when the squeaky-voiced actor was murdered, the bumbling man fell outside the curtain as it dropped. The last sight the audience had was the "corpse" struggling to crawl back underneath the heavy curtain. The play failed miserably and closed after opening night.

William Henry published a confession, much to his father's repugnance. In his confession, William commented upon people's susceptibility to hoaxes: "Once a false idea becomes fixed in a person's mind, he will twist facts or probability to accommodate it rather than question it."

Samuel Ireland continued to believe in the authenticity of

William's forged Shakespeare writings for the rest of his life. In his view, to admit the works were forged would have been to admit he had been fooled by the very son he had declared had neither the intelligence nor the wit to write Shakespeare's plays.

As for William Henry Ireland, if *Vortigern* had succeeded, he planned to double his faked output by forging plays concerning every monarch about whom Shakespeare had not written. However, since both Ireland's forgeries and his theatrical career were short-lived, he settled for writing his own novels and plays, of which he completed over a dozen during his lifetime. None was critically acclaimed, and not one attracted the fame of *Vortigern.*

Who Was the Real Shakespeare?

Many people believe that one phony author may have hoaxed literary experts for centuries. This mystery author's unmasking would enlighten and relieve both literary aficionados and teachers of high school English, all of whom want to know who is the *real* author of Shakespeare's literary works.

Suspects in the mystery have included Sir Francis Bacon, English philosopher and author of *The History of Henry VIII*; Sir Christopher Marlowe, English dramatist credited with writing the second and third parts of *Henry VI* that were allegedly revised by the real Shakespeare; poet Edward de Vere, the seventeenth Earl of Oxford; and the most astounding suspect of all, Queen Elizabeth I. Arguers in favor of Elizabeth claim she was well educated, fluent in seven languages, and wrote poetry that sounded much like Shakespeare's. They speculate that Elizabeth wanted to leave a legacy to England but could not publicly bequest her writings, being a woman and the queen.

Adding to the difficulty in solving the Shakespeare identity is that little is known about him. Authenticated facts include his birth in Stratford-upon-Avon, England, and his occupation as a grain dealer who moonlighted writing plays. There is not one manuscript that can be proven without a doubt to be written in Shakespeare's own hand. Even the spelling of his name is debated. He was baptized "Shakspur" but signed his literary works "Shakespeare."

The quest for the true Shakespeare has been backed by some unexpected sources, such as *Life* magazine, which underwrote an expedition to dig up the floor of Elsinore Castle dungeon. Other Shakespeare scholars are trying to get permission to explore the mysterious mine shafts on Oak Island, off the coast of Nova Scotia, which were dug in Elizabethan times, and where Edward de Vere's lost tomb is supposedly buried. Still others, convinced that the real bard took his identity with him, are trying to get permission to unearth Shakespeare's tomb, allegedly buried seventeen feet beneath his local church in Stratford.

Although the debate continues, the speculators are united by one goal. They need to find one manuscript, in an identifiable handwriting, that will once and for all answer the question: "Shakespeare, Whosoever Art Thou?"

The Howard Hughes Hoax

It just astonished me that anyone could have taken it so seriously.
Clifford Irving

As a novelist turned forger, Clifford Irving remains unique from his counterparts. The most striking difference is that before he faked the autobiography of the billionaire Howard Hughes, Clifford Irving had never forged anything in his life. Irving found the Howard Hughes letters, which he used as a study guide, printed in a news magazine article titled "The Invisible Billionaire." Only after reading this article, did Irving conceive the idea of hoaxing the public by writing a fake Howard Hughes autobiography.

Howard Hughes as a young man.

Howard Hughes.

At the time Irving initiated his hoax there were no biographies written about the secretive Hughes, whom former President Franklin Roosevelt awarded the Congressional Medal of Honor and the Harmon Trophy for his pioneering efforts in aviation. These aviation advances included assembling the world's largest, private air force, and flying around the world in 1939 in one-half the time of Charles Lindbergh. Hughes, who once stated that his four goals in life were to become the richest man, the greatest aviator, the most famous movie producer, and the best golfer in the world, achieved all but his last goal. Hughes' movies *Scarface* and *Hell's Angels* are considered classics, and he is credited with discovering and promoting the acting careers of Jean Harlow and Jane Russell, among others.

Howard Hughes once mingled among statesmen, film executives, and U.S. Presidents. His photograph was on the cover of countless magazines, and stories about him were frequently printed in the press. Then suddenly Howard Hughes went into seclusion, and the public grasped at every rumor concerning his reasons for disappearing and his whereabouts. News reporters hounded his former wives, friends, and business associates for stories about him. After Hughes' mysterious disappearance from public life, he emerged again only once. When Howard Hughes died, his body was brought back from the Bahamas for burial in the United States.

Irving's first step was to forge a letter from Howard Hughes asking him to help write his autobiography. By this action, Irving ranks as the only forger to fake a literary work of a living person. He took a great risk, as Hughes could repudiate the autobiography as soon as it was published. Irving gambled on Hughes' silence. As Howard Hughes had not been seen by anyone other than his personal staff since the late 1950s, Irving figured the man was such a recluse that he would be out of touch with daily news. Thus Hughes would never know the book had been published, much less venture forth from his self-imposed exile—rumored to be on Paradise Island in the Baha-mas—to denounce Irving as a forger.

Irving fantasized "that the book would be so good that Hughes might say, '. . . this is a better life than I've lived!' . . . and let it stand as his autobiography—which was one of the more naive assumptions of the century!"

Irving then convinced his publisher, McGraw Hill, to buy the book, and to pay a $750,000 advance to be split between Hughes and Irving. The contract stipulated that all checks be made payable to H. R. Hughes. Irving's wife Edith, could thus deposit the advance money into a Swiss bank account under the name Helga Renate Hughes. The contract further called for communication only between Clifford Irving and Hughes, in order that McGraw Hill could not contact Hughes and discover the autobiography was a hoax.

Richard Suskind, a fellow writer, and Clifford Irving's friend, joined him as an accomplice. The two men took turns playing Hughes and recorded faked interviews. *Life* magazine offered to buy excerpt rights if the original Hughes letter to Irving was declared genuine. The leading handwriting firm in the United States, Osborn, Osborn, & Osborn, compared the letter to genuine Hughes handwriting and concluded, "The evidence that all of the writing submitted was done by the one individual is . . . irresistible, unanswerable, and overwhelming."

Irving enlisted *Life's* permission to view their files on Hughes. He hid a camera inside his jacket and photographed the files, which contained interviews with Hughes never before printed. Irving intended to include these in his autobiography to give the book a personal touch that would lend credence to its authenticity.

The entire hoax bore a James Bond flavor. For instance, Irving wore gloves when forging letters from Howard Hughes, so as not to leave fingerprints on the paper. He flew around the world, telling his editor at McGraw Hill that he was instructed by Hughes' staff to meet the hermit at bizarre rendezvous points, which he assumed would be typical of Hughes' reclusive personality. On one alleged interview, Irving reported that he was met at an airport in Mexico by a stranger named Pedro, who drove him to a secluded meeting place where "a wreck, a thin and tired ruin" awaited him in a battered Buick. The "ruin" was Howard Hughes. Pedro called the man Octavio. Later, the McGraw Hill staff, wanting to keep the impending Hughes autobiography a secret from other publishers, also began calling Hughes by the code name Octavio.

Clifford Irving developed a genuine talent for forgery, even faking a Swiss passport for his wife to use when depositing McGraw Hill's advance checks. Edith also played the role of feminine spy. Whenever she took the train from Germany to Switzerland, she would sneak into the ladies' room just before the train stopped in Switzerland and don a black wig and dark red lipstick. Then Edith Irving would emerge as Helga Renate Hughes to greet officials at the Credit Suisse Bank.

During the summer of 1971, when Irving and Suskind transcribed their Hughes tapes, the hoax seemed to be filled with lucky coincidences. When Irving visited his aunt in California, he happened to see an old friend, film agent Stanley Meyer. Meyer told Irving that Noah Dietrich, a former aide of Howard Hughes, was collaborating on a biography of Hughes with magazine writer James Phalen. Meyer wanted another writer to re-do the manuscript and offered Irving the job, asking him to read it before giving him an answer. Irving took the manuscript to his hotel room and immediately photocopied it. The next day, he returned the manuscript to Meyer, telling him he was not interested in rewriting it.

Thus Clifford Irving added the crime of plagiarism to forgery. He and Richard Suskind lifted entire paragraphs from the Dietrich manuscript, including a ten-page memo of a telephone conversation between Frank McCulloch, then a reporter for

Time magazine, and Howard Hughes. The billionaire was literally begging McCulloch not to print an article about him. These personal Howard Hughes anecdotes, known only to a few Hughes associates, added to the behind-the-scenes aura of the autobiography.

Lucky coincidences did not prevail indefinitely, however. Irving and Suskind faced several potential discoveries. While telling *Life*'s editor about his "conversations" with Howard Hughes, Irving mentioned that Hughes had known the writer Ernest Hemingway. The *Life* editor answered, "We know Mary Hemingway pretty well. We can ask her about that." Taken aback, Irving quickly responded, "I wonder if Howard ever met her," then made a mental note to make sure he had not.

Then in August, Irving's editor informed him that a man named Sam Post had offered another publisher a book, called *The Autobiography of Howard Hughes*, as told to a man named Robert Eaton. Apparently, Hughes had authorized Eaton in writing to sell his autobiography. Clifford Irving was perhaps the only hoaxer who ever faced competition from an identical hoax! He solved the problem with a forged letter from Hughes authorizing the *specific* publishing company of McGraw Hill to publish his autobiography. In addition, he called the Eaton book a hoax.

Although the contract which Clifford Irving had forged stipulated that no announcement could be made about the autobiography until the book was published, this condition was hastily changed when *Ladies Home Journal* magazine bought excerpt rights to the Eaton book. McGraw Hill felt pressured to announce the Irving/Suskind autobiography before the *Journal* came out with the Eaton excerpts. Irving again solved the problem by forging a letter from Hughes indicating that because of the "Eaton book hoax," he gave McGraw Hill permission to announce his autobiography right away, provided the last advance payment of $350,000 was made simultaneously.

(Irving and Suskind feared the announcement might draw skepticism as to the autobiography's authenticity, causing Mc-Graw Hill to halt payment of the final advance.)

Taking that precaution proved a wise move, as practically the minute McGraw Hill made the announcement, the supports under the Irving and Suskind hoax began to crumble. When writer James Phalen heard about a passage in the Irving autobiography that only Hughes' aid Noah Dietrich could have known, he accused Irving and Suskind of plagiarism. McGraw Hill asked Osborn, Osborn, & Osborn to recompare the original Hughes letter to Irving with the genuine Hughes letter found in the news magazine. This time, the Osborns spotted differences in the two handwriting samples they had previously missed. Irving's "b's" started too high above the line, his "p's" were executed with one continuous stroke instead of the two used by Hughes, and under a magnifying glass previously hidden pen lifts between letters were seen. The Osborns reversed their former opinion and declared Irving's letter a forgery.

Chipping away another piece of the Howard Hughes hoax, investigators in Switzerland managed to break the time-honored code of anonymity in Swiss bank accounts and discovered that the real Helga R. Hughes was Edith Irving.

The greatest blow to Irving and Suskind came from the most unexpected source. For the first time in years, Howard Hughes spoke out. He told his aides he wanted to talk, via a speaker telephone, to Frank McCulloch, now *Time* magazine's bureau chief, and the last person to have interviewed Hughes. Six other reporters, who on earlier occasions had interviewed Howard Hughes and who therefore could recognize his voice, also sat in on the conversation.

After listening to the speaker on the other end of the voice box, McCulloch told Irving, "I have to tell you . . . that to the best of my knowledge that was Hughes I spoke to. His voice is unmistakable, as I'm sure you know." Irving asked, "What did Hughes say?" To which McCulloch answered, "Among other things, that he'd never met anyone named Clifford Irving in his whole life."

Richard Suskind, Edith Irving, and Clifford Irving were charged with fraud and grand larceny. On June 16, 1972, Edith Irving was fined ten thousand dollars and given a two-year prison sentence. For the sake of their children, all except two months of her sentence was to be served on probation. However, she eventually served time in prison in Switzerland for fraudulently opening a bank account there.

Richard Suskind was sentenced to six months in a New York State prison for being an accomplice to fraud.

Clifford Irving was given a two-and-a-half-year prison sentence and fined ten thousand dollars. In 1983, he still owed one million dollars in debts from his hoax attempt.

CHAPTER FIVE

MEDIA HOAXES

The great problem is at length solved! The air, as well as the earth and the ocean, has been subdued by science and will become a common and convenient highway for mankind! The Atlantic has actually been crossed in a Balloon!

This headline amazed the world on April 13, 1844. Printed in the *New York Sun*, the story claimed that the *Victoria*, a British balloon, had flown from Europe to America and landed at Sullivan's Island, near Charleston, South Carolina. The historic journey had taken seventy-five hours.

The *Sun*'s reporter detailed his "hot exclusive" with sketches of the balloon's structure, excerpts from the flight log, plus gossip and quotes from the celebrated passengers. Given special mention was the noted British aeronaut, Monck Mason, famous for his forty-four-foot model airship, or dirigible, as it was called, which was driven by clockwork and flown in circles around a Paris gallery.

The publisher of the *Sun* was so intrigued by the story that he told his city editor to locate the article's reporter and find out more about the historic event. The city editor uncovered more than the publisher bargained for. The *Victoria* never landed in South Carolina, or anywhere else. The amazing balloon was amazing only in the reporter's imagination.

Broke and owing enormous bills for his sick wife, the reporter needed money desperately. When he heard the news from Paris of Monck Mason's fantastic model dirigible, it gave him the idea of inventing his own balloon story, then selling it to the *Sun* to earn a welcome paycheck.

Thus the great balloon hoax was born. The publisher of the *Sun* stormed at the city editor for not verifying his facts before buying the front page exclusive and decreed that the reporter would never again have his news features printed in the *Sun*.

"Who is this crazy fellow?" fumed the publisher.

"Chap named Poe," the city editor responded.

Edgar Allan Poe, known later as a writer of mystery stories such as "The Fall of the House of Usher" and "The Gold Bug," was then a young reporter with a vivid imagination.

Journalists in 1844, as well as those before and since, have known that unusual or exciting news attracts readers and that front page scoops increase newspaper sales as well as the fame of the writer. Thus, when sensational news is not available, the temptation may be to embroider the news with exciting, but invented, details.

When, for instance, the tomb of King Tutankhamen was opened in February, 1923, reporter Charles Langden Clark wrote an article for the *Toronto Mail and Empire* entitled "King Tut's Golden Typewriter." The archeologists who discovered the tomb had previously agreed to give exclusive rights to print the story to the *Times* of London. Not being among the privileged reporters did not deter Clark. He simply added his own details to already published information. Only after a rival editor checked with an Egyptology expert did Clark reveal his hoax.

SATURDAY, APRIL 13, 1844.

SUN OFFICE,
April 13, 1844—half 2 A. M.

ASTOUNDING NEWS!

BY EXPRESS VIA NORFOLK!

THE

ATLANTIC CROSSED

IN

THREE DAYS!

SIGNAL TRIUMPH

OF

MR. MONCK MASON'S

FLYING

MACHINE!!!

Arrival at Sullivan's Island, near Charleston, S. C., of Mr. Mason, Mr. Robert Holland, Mr. Henson, Mr. Harrison Ainsworth, and four others, in the

STEERING BALLOON

"VICTORIA,"

AFTER A PASSAGE OF

SEVENTY-FIVE HOURS

FROM LAND TO LAND.

FULL PARTICULARS

OF THE

VOYAGE!!!

THE MODEL.

OF THE VICTORIA.

Edgar Allan Poe, perpetrator of the "Balloon Hoax".

Today, journalists are expected to use reputable sources and to verify stories before putting them into print. Readers take personal offense if a story presented as fact turns out to be untrue. For instance, when it was revealed in 1981 that a Pulitzer Prize-winning reporter for the *Washington Post* had invented the main characters of her story about drug abuse among children, there was a huge public outcry.

In the nineteenth century, the relative slowness of communication and transportation made it difficult to confirm questionable information. Thus, a newspaper editor fearing a scoop by a competing paper might print a story and check its facts later.

Nearly seventy-five years after the balloon hoax story appeared, a similar tale was published. However, by then it was a simple matter to check the details quickly by telephone and telegraph. A popular magazine called *Flying* had reported that a man named Alfred E. Poor had flown nonstop in his airplane

Front page of the New York Sun *announcing the cross Atlantic flight of the balloon* Victoria.

from Newfoundland to Ireland on July 28 and 29, 1918. The article included illustrations, a map of the route, and a navigator's log. Had the flight been real, it would have been historic—the first solo flight across the Atlantic. However, as the editors promptly confessed, the story was a hoax. They claimed they had published it in order to stimulate further efforts by aviators to accomplish this challenging feat.

The Great Wall Hoax

In 1899, four newspaper reporters in Denver, Colorado, sat having coffee at the Hotel Oxford. Tired and frustrated, they were at a loss for a news story to turn into their editors for the next morning's edition. One reporter suggested that if they could not find a good story, they should invent one. Another reporter replied that if they were going to invent the news, they should invent a whopper of a story. Thus was born the Great Wall hoax, a deception that had more far-reaching results than those bored, tired newspaper reporters ever imagined.

As a collaborative hoax, each reporter sent in the story that plans were underway for a team of American demolition experts to knock down and then rebuild a portion of the Great Wall of China. Their phony front page headlines astounded Denverites for a few days, then were relegated to the back pages. However, two weeks later, the story resurfaced in a newspaper on the East Coast, complete with illustrations, political analyses of the Chinese government's reactions to the American government's intentions, and quotes from a Chinese visitor to New York who confirmed the report.

Like the childhood game of Telephone, in which one person whispers a message to another player in a circle and that player whispers the message to the next until the last person speaks the message out loud, usually in a garbled version, by the time the Great Wall story reached China, the American demolitioners had turned into "invaders who intended to destroy the entire historical monument."

Violent repercussions followed. The Chinese were already upset by foreign intervention into their provinces. One segment of the population opposed all Western cultural influences. They formed a secret society called the Order of Literary Patriotic Harmonious Fists to verbally attack western businessmen visiting China. When the headlines reported America's intention to destroy the Great Wall, the news ignited the sparks of Chinese discontent with foreign intervention into a blazing bonfire.

America's denials of the story were ignored by the secret society. In June, 1900, the Harmonious Fists instigated a national rebellion in which many Chinese citizens were horribly killed. Members also took control of the foreign embassies in Peking and murdered hundreds of missionaries.

An international army of French, British, American, German, Russian, and Japanese troops invaded China. In Peking, troops looted the Emperor's palace and slaughtered thousands of Chinese without caring whether or not they belonged to the Harmonious Fists. Upon suppressing the rebellion, the invaders forced China to pay an indemnity of three hundred twenty million dollars.

Some political scientists still speculate whether the Harmonious Fists would have rebelled regardless of the reporters' hoax. Others maintain that Chinese history might have been entirely different if not for the four reporters who met that Saturday night at the Hotel Oxford in Denver.

Today American high school students may not read about the reporters' hoax in their history books. But they will read about the violent Chinese rebellion that occurred in 1900 that was named after the Order of Literary Patriotic Harmonious Fists, otherwise known as the Boxer Rebellion.

The Wild Animal Hoax

Many of the best newspaper hoaxes were created in the nineteenth century. Journalists then enjoyed much greater freedom in their reporting. They were able to be much more imaginative, and it was difficult for the reader to discern the fine line between fact and fiction in their stories. Although clues to invented facts might be provided, they might not be obvious after a quick reading, or might not appear until the end of the story.

For instance, when in 1874 the managing editor of the New York *Herald* wanted to attract the public's attention to the shortcomings of the Central Park Zoo, he decided that the best way to do it would be to first report an imaginary scenario in which all the animals escaped and terrorized the city. Then he would outline how the zoo needed to be improved to prevent such an event from ever happening.

The article, which came to be known as the Wild Animal Hoax, began with an eyewitness account describing the escape of all the animals in the zoo. As a result, the article claimed, forty-nine persons were dead and two hundred injured. The mayor himself warned all citizens to stay safely at home! The story continued by saying that leading citizens were participating in an animal hunt and that twelve animals were still at large.

Many people, including the owner of the newspaper, James Gordon Bennett, never reached the end of the article to read the paragraph that revealed the story as a fabrication. It is said that while reading the story Mr. Bennett collapsed in his bed and stayed there all day!

The wild animal hoax was not intended as such, but rather to raise the public's consciousness about an important community issue. Recently, Alan Abel, a practical joker whose autobiography is titled *Confessions of a Hoaxer,* used the media to create another fake news event in order to call attention to his own cause, known as FAINT (Fight Against Idiotic Neurotic Television).

In January, 1985, during a live broadcast of the Phil Donahue talk show, Abel orchestrated fake fainting fits by six people in the studio audience. Studio personnel rushed to their aid, medical help was summoned, and the "victims" sent home in cabs. Not only did the fainting episode reach the normal television audience of the Donahue show, but it was broadcast later on the evening news. After the hoax was revealed, Alan Abel apologized for having used the Donahue show and said it was chosen only because it was one of the few live broadcasts

Practical joker, Alan Abel, displaying the "official" magazine of his bogus organization, The Society for Indecency to Naked Animals.

available for such a stunt. Abel claimed his purpose in staging the event was to encourage live television, protest poor-quality television, and generally "raise the subconscious of the public by going unconscious."

Alan Abel has played many such jokes on the public. In 1959 he wrote to television's *Today Show* concerning his alleged organization, the Society for Indecency to Naked Animals. He signed the letter with the invented name, G. Clifford Trout, Jr., president, and added his own name as vice-president. The producers then asked both men to appear on the *Today Show*. Abel asked a friend, Buck Henry, to appear with him and pretend to be the president of the society. On the show, Henry stated, "Don't let your moral standards go lower and lower due to naked animals. It's a shocking situation, and I am spending . . . every last dollar of my father's money to correct this evil."

The two hoaxers were pursued for more interviews, including one with *Life* magazine in which Abel's friends brought their dogs appropriately clothed. The hoax was revealed three years later when Buck Henry began to work at CBS and someone at the television station recognized him.

The Moon Hoax

One of the most imaginative and celebrated newspaper hoaxes ever perpetrated was a series of articles published in the New York *Sun* in August, 1835. Supposedly reprinted from a supplement to the Edinburgh *Journal of Science*, the articles detailed the discovery of life on the moon by the noted astronomer Sir John Herschel. It was reported that through his giant telescope, which he had installed on the southern tip of Africa at the Cape of Good Hope, Sir John and his assistants were able to view the surface of the moon so clearly that it seemed as if the moon were only one hundred yards away. The astronomers allegedly saw a great inland sea with a beach of "brilliant white

Artist's view of life on the moon according to the report published in the New York Sun, *August, 1835 (from an old print).*

sand" on which were plants, animals, and even humanlike creatures with wings. It was all described in glowing detail:

> We counted three parties of these creatures, of twelve, nine, and fifteen in each, walking erect towards a small wood. . . . Certainly they were like human beings, for their wings had now disappeared and their attitude in walking was both erect and dignified. . . .
>
> . . . They averaged four feet in height, were covered, except on the face, with short and glossy copper-colored hair, and had wings composed of a thin membrane, without hair, lying snugly upon their backs from the top of the shoulders to the calves of the legs.
>
> The face, which was of a yellowish flesh color, was a slight improvement upon that of the large orangutan. . . . The hair on the head was a darker color than that of the body, closely curled but apparently not wooly, and arranged in two curious semi-circles over the temples of the forehead. Their feet could only be

seen as they were alternately lifted in walking; but from what we could see of them in so transient a view, they appeared thin and very protuberant at the heel.

Even though the first article about Herschel's discoveries appeared without any special fanfare headlines, it instantly caught the imagination of the public. When the fourth article in the moon series appeared, the editor of the *Sun*, Benjamin Day, claimed that his newspaper had the largest circulation of any in the world. Every other newspaper in New York and elsewhere was desperate to obtain material about life on the moon. Some of them, unable to find a copy of the *Journal of Science*, simply reprinted the articles that had appeared in the *Sun*. At the same time, a group of scientists from Yale University, also looking for the *Journal of Science* articles, came to New York to inspect those at the *Sun* office. The scientists were led on a wild goose chase from editorial office to print shop and back, and, of course, never found the articles, as they had never existed in the first place. Finally, a *Sun* reporter, Richard Adams Locke, confessed to being the author of the moon story, claiming it had been intended as a satire. On September 16, 1835, the newspaper publicly admitted the hoax.

Today, via television, we have seen earthly men fly to the moon and walk on its surface wearing space suits, so that to think anyone would have believed the amazing descriptions reported in Locke's moon story seems ridiculous. Some parts of the story were based on fact, however, and this lent the fantastic aspects some credibility.

For instance, there had once been a publication called the *Journal of Science* in Edinburgh, although by 1835 it was no longer in business. It certainly did not ever contain any account of life on the moon though. Also, Locke's knowledge of astronomy was sufficient enough that his use of terminology was genuine in some cases, and in others had the ring of truth.

Sir John Herschel was, in fact, a well-known, highly re-

spected astronomer who by 1835 had made significant astronomical discoveries, including the identification of many double
stars and nebulae. With his father, Sir Frederick Herschel, he
had constructed, and then later improved, a large, reflecting
telescope. In 1834 he decided to take his telescope to the Cape
of Good Hope to observe the southern constellations. Although
his telescope was large by the standards of the day—twenty-feet
long, with an eighteen-inch diameter—it was nowhere near the
dimensions described in the newspaper story. The fictitious
telescope supposedly had a lens twenty-four feet in diameter,
which weighed 14,826 pounds!

Perhaps another reason the public was so willing to accept
the moon hoax was that equally strange but true stories about
creatures and plants could be found here on earth. If exotic
wildlife and people with strange appearances and customs could
be found in newly explored regions of Africa, India, South
America, and Australia, then why not on the moon? In fact, a
group of Baptist clergymen full of missionary zeal wrote to Sir
John Herschel to ask if there might be a means of sending word
of the Gospel to the residents of the moon.

After the moon story was exposed as a hoax, it continued to
spread and was even translated into other languages. Showmen
reproduced the story in dioramas for exhibition, and elaborate
stage productions were created. The moon hoax was too fascinating to die of its own accord. A letter written by Lady
Herschel to her husband's aunt suggests why so many people
were intrigued by the moon hoax:

> The whole description is so well clenched with minute details
> of workmanship and names of individuals boldly referred to, that
> the New Yorkists were not to be blamed for actually believing it
> as they did for forty-eight hours. It is only a great pity that it is
> not true.

Only after Sir John Herschel himself signed a statement
denying the story was the moon hoax finally put to rest.

Mark Twain's Nevada Newspaper Hoaxes

Samuel Clemens, known better by his pseudonym Mark Twain, is one of the leading writers of American fiction. Yet, it was his talent for fiction that got him into serious trouble as a young newspaper reporter instructed to report the facts. Never content to present dull information, Twain often embellished or simply created his own stories.

When Mark Twain left his home on the Mississippi in 1861 to travel west to Nevada with his brother, Orion, his goal was to strike it rich by mining gold and silver. Instead, he discovered a tough life in bleak surroundings and no fortune. In his spare time he wrote short comical letters, which he sent to the local newspaper, the Virginia City *Territorial Enterprise*. To his surprise, the paper printed them. These letters, such as his story about a Professor Personal Pronoun, were spoofs on local characters and brought him to the attention of the *Enterprise*'s editor, who offered him a job on the paper.

Twain began work at the *Enterprise* in September, 1862, and only two weeks later wrote his petrified man hoax, a story aimed at making fun of what he felt was the "growing evil" of the mania for digging up "petrifactions." Twain later wrote "I chose to kill the petrifaction mania with a delicate, a very delicate satire."

According to Twain's story, a petrified figure of a seated man had been discovered embedded in a cliff near a place known as Gravelly Ford. He described the figure in minute detail and added that one leg had been replaced by a wooden one. At the inquest, he wrote, it was determined by a Justice Sewell that death had been caused by "protracted exposure."

For local readers, certain details, such as the fact that there was no Justice Sewell, and other inaccuracies made it obvious that the article was a joke. Citizens in other communities however, apparently found the story plausible, and newspapers all over the United States, and even some abroad, reprinted it.

Mark Twain in 1864, as a reporter on the Virginia City Enterprise.

When Mark Twain realized the success of his story, he wrote a follow-up and added even more outrageous details. According to this tall tale, an assayer had supposedly taken a small amount of dirt found under the petrified nail of the man's big toe, analyzed it, and determined that the man had been a "native of the Kingdom of New Jersey." Anyone who wished to see the remains of the petrified man, added Twain, was invited to come to the library where the petrified remains had been placed on view in a glass case. How many people visited the library to see the nonexistent remains was not recorded, but no doubt there was more than one gullible reader.

About a year later, in October, 1863, Twain imposed another wild story on the readers of the *Enterprise*. According to this story, which became known as the bloody massacre, a man named P. Hopkins, having learned that his investments in a

Virginia City mining company had been lost, exploded in a mad rage and brutally murdered his wife and seven of his nine children. The story described the murders in graphic detail and then said that Hopkins, his throat cut from ear to ear, had jumped on his horse and ridden into town clutching the red-haired scalp of his wife. There, in front of the town saloon, he died.

Again, for those who lived in the area, there were many clues in the story giving it away as a fabrication. The story claimed that Hopkins and his family lived "in the old log house just to the edge of the great pine forest which lies between Empire City and Dutch Nick's." However, Empire City and Dutch Nick's were actually the same place, and there was no pine forest in that area, no log house, and no large Hopkins family. Another Virginia City newspaper saw through the story immediately and rebuked the author: "Now we go in for any and all men writing for the press drawing on their imaginations—when they have any—but we are not an admirer of foundationless yarns full of horror, and which by mentioning names and localities, may do much injury without the probability of doing good."

Many other newspapers throughout the West reprinted all or parts of the bloody massacre story. When Twain retracted the story the following day, the newspapers that had printed it were furious. One wrote, "The ass who originated the story doubtless thinks he is 'old smarty'—we don't." The San Francisco *Journal* commented, "We are not fond of hoaxing our readers, and hereby give the *Enterprise* notice that as long as they keep the author of that hoax in their employ, we shall not trouble their columns for news matter."

Despite the uproar, Mark Twain did not lose his job. However, later that year, when the *Enterprise* printed a true story of a man who had run amok and stabbed four men in the town of Gold Hill, no one believed it. Neither did they believe a story about a miner who had been attacked by wolves. The public was wary of being fooled once again.

Mark Twain's last Nevada hoax revolved around raising money for an organization called The United States Sanitary Commission, a private philanthropic group that was a predecessor of the Red Cross. In many cities, money was raised by giving a Sanitary Fair, which was sometimes accompanied by a fancy dress ball. Another technique for raising funds was originated by a politician named Ruel C. Gridley. On a bet, Gridley carried a fifty-pound sack of flour between the towns of Austin and Clifton. Then he auctioned off the sack of flour and gave the proceeds to the Sanitary Fund. The sack was then auctioned by each new owner until a great deal of money had been raised. This money was added to the money collected at the town's Sanitary Fair and Ball.

One night, as Mark Twain sat in the newspaper office with a fellow reporter, Dan De Quille, he scribbled a short article, in jest, which suggested that the money collected at a recent Sanitary Ball was being "diverted from its legitimate course." Then, on second thought, Twain decided that his joke was in poor taste and tossed it aside. Unfortunately, when Twain and De Quille left, the composing room foreman found the article on the table, assumed it was copy for the next day's paper, and printed it. In the uproar that followed, Twain exchanged irate words with James L. Laird, proprietor of the *Union* which was a rival newspaper, which resulted in the threat of a duel between them. In the end no duel was fought, but Mark Twain soon left Virginia City to become a reporter for the San Francisco *Call*.

CHAPTER SIX

FAMOUS IMPOSTORS

Stanley Weinberg, the son of poor immigrants living in Brooklyn, wanted to rise above his station in life. First, he changed his name to Stanley Weyman. Then he impersonated a doctor, university professor, U.S. Navy lieutenant-commander, and a Romanian consul general. When the famous silent film star Rudolph Valentino died, Weyman posed as the star's doctor, assisted with the funeral arrangements and became the personal physician of Valentino's frequent costar, Pola Negri. Another time, Weyman posed as the State Department's chief protocol officer and escorted Princess Fatima of Afghanistan to Washington for a meeting with then President Warren G. Harding.

History is filled with people who played the part of another to achieve their own goals. A successful impostor must be an historian, an actor, and an improvisationist all at the same time. Hours are spent researching every detail about the impersonated person's life. Even obscure, minor childhood incidents must be discovered and memorized. The impostor cannot hesitate when asked questions by relatives or friends. A stumbling explanation or an "I can't remember" rouses suspicions. If the impostor blunders, he or she must be capable of improvising a believable explanation for the error.

To actively incorporate another's identity into one's own and literally *become* that person for a long period of time, the impostor must squelch his or her own identity. History and literature are filled with accounts of impostors who found themselves really becoming the person they impersonated. In 1905, Father Gapon, a police spy for the Russian government, helped to start the Russian Revolution by *actually becoming* the workers' leader he pretended to be.

George Psalmanazar

Fame, fortune, and the need to hide his real identity were the motivating forces behind George Psalmanazar's imposture. Little is known about the man except his birth date sometime between 1679 and 1694 in southern France, and his education, which was by Jesuit priests.

In 1701, while enlisted in the Lutheran regiment of the Duke of Mecklenberg, Psalmanazar posed as Japanese. The army chaplain, a Reverend William Innes, realized Psalmanazar's ruse when he questioned him about life in Japan and found Psalmanazar extremely lacking in knowledge of even the most everyday Japanese customs. Innes, being a dishonest and ambitious adventurer himself, offered to arrange Psalmanazar's discharge from the army and take him to London. The Reverend suggested that Psalmanazar pose as a native of a more obscure land, since English merchants and seamen had visited Japan and would know the people's history and customs. After much thought, the two hoaxers decided upon Formosa.

They returned to England, where the "Native of Formosa"

became an overnight social success. He was entertained by royalty—even the Archbishop of Canterbury praised his grasp of the English language. Since his audiences had never been to Formosa, his lectures on life in the strange, exotic land kept them spellbound. Psalmanazar found it easy to make up stories. For example, he said that most Formosans lived to be one hundred, and that gold and silver were abundant there. The "Native of Formosa" feigned bizarre Formosan customs, such as wearing a snake draped around his neck "to keep him cool."

Knowing the British were fascinated by stories of cannibalism, Psalmanazar regaled them with gruesome customs, such as when a man wished to divorce his wife, he cut off her head, then ate her remains. "I think it no sin to eat human flesh," he admitted, "but I must own that it is a little unmannerly."

When asked why his skin and complexion were fair, instead of yellowish like most Orientals, Psalmanazar said he belonged to the upper-class Formosans, who lived in "cool shades or apartments underground," while the lower classes labored in the sun, which tanned their skin a yellowish tint.

In 1704 Psalmanazar wrote a book titled *An Historical and Geographical Description of Formosa*, containing a "Formosan alphabet and grammar," and describing the land's religion, customs, and economics. Grammar experts have called Psalmanazar's alphabet "one of the best artificial languages ever invented . . . well suited to everyday use." Many historical authorities consider his book the finest work of historical and geographical fiction ever written.

Psalmanazar played his masquerade for twenty-five years. However, like many impostors with overinflated imaginations, he did not know when to quit. His hoax was exposed when he wrote a sequel to his first book and included even more bizarre Formosan customs, which the public found too incredible to believe. Edmund Halley, the distinguished astronomer, questioned Psalmanazar about astronomical phenomena in Formosa. Psalmanazar's answers were totally incorrect. Sir Isaac Newton publicly denounced the "Formosan" as a fraud, charging that portions of his Formosan history were plagiarized from texts on Formosa and Japan published in England forty years previously.

Psalmanazar confessed his hoax and lived in poverty until his death in 1763, at the age of eighty-four. His memoirs reveal the true story of his imposture, with one exception—his real name. To the world, the man with the mysterious, unknown past will forever be George Psalmanazar, "Native of Formosa."

George Psalmanazar's twenty-five-year masquerade was judged so astounding by the *National Review* magazine that the editors created an annual award after him. The George Psalmanazar Award is given each year to the best hoaxer of the year.

In 1972, the editors could not decide between two hoaxers. They voted therefore to give two awards that year—one to Clifford Irving, for his fake autobiography of Howard Hughes, and the other to Chief Red Fox, a Sioux Indian. The latter's forged book, *Memoirs of Chief Red Fox,* was praised by both the *New York Times* and Richard Nixon, then president of the United States. The book was discovered to be a hoax when the Sioux claimed no Chief Red Fox was ever a member of their tribe. It was soon revealed that Red Fox had lifted almost twelve thousand words from a thirty-year-old history of the Sioux, known by historians to be genuine. The Chief claimed he did not care about his being charged with fraud and boasted, "I already have enough money [from the sale of his book], to set my tombstone up."

Sarah Wilson

Shortly before the American Revolution, Sarah Wilson, a maid at the palace of Queen Charlotte and King George III of England, tried to raise her servant's lot in life by stealing the queen's jewelry, clothes and other belongings. She was caught in the act by another chambermaid. She was tried, found guilty, and sentenced to life in the American colonies. Once there, she ran away from her Maryland plantation owner.

Sarah dressed herself in an elegant outfit she had secretly kept from the queen and took on the identity of "Princess Susanna Carolina Matilda," younger sister of Queen Charlotte. One reason Sarah's imposture succeeded was that she had learned how to behave like a princess while working at the palace. Sarah was an adept actress and used her talents to move and speak with the air of royalty. Sarah the "princess" carried off her imposture for eighteen months, while the wealthy families of the South entertained her as a guest in their homes.

Eventually the slaveowner located Sarah and brought her back to Maryland. She remained in his service until the outbreak of the Revolutionary War, when, taking advantage of the confusion, she ran away once again. This time she headed North, met a British army officer, Lieutenant William Talbot, and eventually married him. After the war, the couple moved to New York where they became one of the wealthiest families in town. Thus Sarah Wilson, portraying herself, finally attained the high social and financial position she had sought so long in the role of impostor.

Cassie Chadwick

Almost one hundred years later, another woman, also motivated by desires of wealth and grandeur, turned to the crime of imposture. Constance Cassandra Chadwick, nicknamed Cassie, was born in Toronto, Canada, in 1845. She was blessed with brains, beauty, and nerve, but no money. In her teens, Cassie ran away to New York City and learned enough by studying books to convince educated people that she was well-versed in art, literature, and world events.

One day she saw a newspaper article about steel magnate

Andrew Carnegie, which noted, "Just the mention of Andrew Carnegie's name is sufficient to prompt any banker in the world to open his vaults." Cassie decided to use Andrew Carnegie's name to open vaults for herself. She read everything she could find about Carnegie. She memorized details of his life, including his charitable donations, such as establishing more than twenty-eight hundred libraries in the United States. Cassie discovered that the billionaire was only five-feet-six-inches tall and had ordered the doors in his mansion constructed so that only short people could pass through without bending over.

Having completed her homework, Cassie prepared for her debut as an impostor. She "let it slip" to a prominent investment broker that she was an intimate friend of Andrew Carnegie, who shared his investment plans with her. She duped the broker into believing Carnegie had given her twelve million dollars in stock certificates as a gift, instructing her to invest a portion of the certificates and save the rest.

The broker figured he had discovered an eternal gold mine in Cassie Chadwick. When she announced she was saving seven million dollars of the certificates, the man took her to a bank to deposit the fortune in a vault. He was so taken by Cassie's charm that he did not even check the envelope's contents before locking up the alleged certificates.

Cassie then used her "Carnegie connection" and her nonexistent securities as collateral to borrow money. Her *modus operandi* was to get a loan from one bank, then another from a second bank to pay off the first. In this way, Cassie pocketed a fortune from banks all along the East Coast. She invested some of the borrowed money in stocks, planning to use the interest to pay off her loans if the stocks increased in value.

In the meantime, Cassie traveled across America relishing her success and spending her borrowed fortune freely. Cassie's imposture might have continued indefinitely had the stock market not crashed at the turn of the century. Her stocks plummeted, and the banks called in her loans. By this time, however, Cassie had spent all her borrowed money. The banks demanded she use the seven million dollars that she had put in the bank vault as collateral to clear her debts. Upon opening the vault, both the investment broker and the banks' loan officers were shocked. Nothing but newspaper clippings were inside the envelope allegedly containing the money. Many of the articles were about Andrew Carnegie. When the steel magnate's attorneys were questioned, they informed the bankers that Andrew Carnegie had never even met a lady named Cassie Chadwick.

During Cassie's subsequent trial for imposture and fraud, the prosecution learned she had bilked some of the most respected banks along the eastern seaboard of more than fifty million dollars. Cassie showed no remorse and declared her imposture was "a dream come true. If I had the opportunity, I would live that dream again. . . ."

Cassie was found guilty and sentenced to eight years in prison. The hard life took its toll on her. Before she had served two years of her sentence, Constance Cassandra Chadwick lay on her prison cot one night, turned toward the stone wall, and died.

Phony Royalty

Most children have at times wished to be a king or queen just like the people they read about in fairy tales. Children usually grow up and out of their Cinderella fantasies. Some never do. For these people, faking the winning "royalty" ticket in life's birthright lottery seems a small crime in comparison to a lifetime of being cast in the role of commoner.

Whenever a monarch, an heir to the throne, or an inheritor of titled nobility dies in circumstances in which his or her body cannot be found or identified, impostors pop out of the woodwork and return from shipwrecks, assassinations, dungeons, and battlegrounds. As Shakespeare said, "How oft the sight of the means to do ill deeds /Makes ill deeds done."

In the middle 1800s in England, Roger Charles Tichbourne, of the prosperous, respected Tichbourne family, fell in love with his first cousin, Katherine Doughty. When the couple wanted to marry, their families objected. Both sets of parents agreed, however, that if after three years the couple still wanted to marry, they would give Roger and Katherine their blessings. To make the time pass more quickly, Roger sailed around the world. He left Katherine a letter saying that when they married, he promised to build a chapel to the Virgin in thanksgiving. Katherine wrote a copy for herself, then Roger gave the original to his best friend, Vincent Gosport.

Tragically, in April, 1854, Roger's ship, the *Bella*, sank in a storm off the coast of Brazil, and all passengers were supposedly drowned. Lady Tichbourne, however, never accepted her son Roger's death and advertised in newspapers for information of his whereabouts.

Eleven years later, in Wagga Wagga, Australia, a butcher named Arthur Orton, read one of the advertisements and wrote Lady Tichbourne claiming to be her son Roger. Lady Tichbourne was so overjoyed to get her son back after such a long time she accepted Orton's story without question and sent him money for passage to England.

Once established in the Tichbourne family, Arthur Orton initiated proceedings to claim Roger's inheritance. A hearing was held in spite of protests from Lady Tichbourne, who swore Orton was her son. The hearing lasted one hundred and two days, during which time Orton presented an elaborate tale about how he was rescued from the sea by Australians, and about how he settled in Australia. Although Orton greatly resembled Roger Tichbourne, and was a good enough actor to convince almost everyone he was Roger, Orton was not adept at improvisation—a crucial tool of the impostor. When asked to explain how he could be raised in France, yet speak no French,

Arthur Orton had no explanation. Neither could he remember the name of even one boyhood friend or teacher from Roger's boarding school. The evidence mounted against Orton. Furthermore, he had no explanation as to what happened to the initials "R.T." tatooed on the real Roger's arm. Another incriminating piece of evidence against Orton was his failure to know what was written in the letter Roger had given Vincent Gosport and Katherine Doughty.

The claimant was charged with fraud and perjury and many people in England divided into sides over the case. The trial which followed lasted one hundred and eighty-eight days, and was the longest trial in British history at that time. Arthur Orton was found guilty and sentenced to fourteen years in prison. His alleged imposture cost both the British government and the Tichbourne family a fortune.

Lady Tichbourne never stopped believing that Arthur Orton was her son. Added to this unsettling premise—that a mother should be able to recognize her son—was that in all the testimony from the trial, there was no explanation as to Orton's knowing intimate details about the Tichbourne family. Author Geddes MacGregor, in his book *The Tichbourne Impostor*, speculates that somehow Roger Tichbourne had survived the shipwreck and did go to Australia. While there, Roger committed a crime for which he was imprisoned for those eleven years between the shipwreck and Roger's answer to his mother's advertisement. He could have forgotten many details from his life before he sailed. Supporting this theory is the fact that up until his death, the claimant recalled more and more anecdotes of Roger Tichbourne's early life, which only the real Roger could have known.

The Tichbourne imposture has been called the most expensive, complicated, and puzzling case in British jurisprudence. When the claimant was paroled in 1884, he still insisted he was the real Roger Tichbourne and went by that name until his death in 1898. At least one other person must have continued to believe the claimant was Roger Tichbourne also. For on Arthur Orton's tombstone is inscribed, "Sir Roger Charles Doughty Tichbourne."

The False Dauphins

Fantasies of royalty are fairly common. At one time, thirty-two men all claimed to be Louis XVII, son and heir to the throne of the last Bourbon King of France, Louis XVI. When King Louis XVI and his wife, Marie Antoinette, were beheaded in 1793 during the French Revolution, their daughter, the princess royale, and son, the dauphin, were imprisoned for eighteen months, during which time they never saw daylight. Their meals were shoved through the grate in the prison door. Supposedly the dauphin, then eleven years old, died of scurvy in June, 1795, while his sister survived.

Rumors abounded, however, that the dauphin had been smuggled out of France by Bourbon sympathizers and another child substituted in his place. Years later, impostors regularly appeared at the palace gates, each with an incredible tale of intrigue concerning his rescue from prison and his life since 1795. So popular were the impostors' tales that the American author Mark Twain even wrote one into his book *The Adventures of Huckleberry Finn*.

In 1818, making a dramatic appearance as the lost dauphin, was Henri Hebert of Austria. In fabricating his tale of how he came to be the lost dauphin, Hebert modified and personalized the Trojan Horse story. He claimed that another child was drugged and hidden inside a toy horse, which was then rolled into his prison cell. Hebert was then put inside the horse and rolled out of the cell to freedom. Hebert also fabricated a "Gulliverian" travelogue, which included staying with a strange tribe of people called the "Mamelucks," to account for the years since his escape. Henri Hebert was eventually arrested for imposture in 1833 and sentenced to twelve years imprisonment.

The only lost dauphin claimant to be given any credence was an American missionary, Reverend Eleazar Williams. Supposedly, two strange men brought a sick young boy to the home of a St. Regis Indian, named Thomas Williams, living in New York. Thomas named the boy Eleazar and raised him as his own. Eleazar had no memory of his early life until the Prince of Joinville, the son of then King of France, Louis Philippe, visited him when he was an adult missionary in Green Bay, Wisconsin. The prince was struck by Eleazar's Bourbon features. And the fact that Williams bore scars identical to those known to be on Louis XVII's body revealed that Eleazar was in fact the dauphin. He had been rescued by friends who substituted the body of another child in the dauphin's place. Upon questioning, Eleazar remembered a scene from his childhood of a lady with a fancy dress and train and appeared frightened when the prince showed him a picture of Simon, the dauphin's jailer.

Eleazar Williams, one of many claimants to the French throne.

The Prince of Joinville was next in line for the throne upon Louis Philippe's death—if the missing dauphin did not return to France and claim the monarchy. Therefore, the prince persuaded Williams to sign a statement of abdication, in return for which Eleazar would be given a lifelong pension from the

Marker near Green Bay, Wisconsin, honoring the site of Eleazar William's home.

Marker reads:

This table marks the landed estate of Eleazar Williams who served in the U.S.A. during the War of 1812 and who was reputed to be Louis XVII, Dauphin of France. This tract of land extending from Little Rapids to Kaukauna was deeded by Menominee Indians to Madeline Jordain, a daughter of the tribe and wife of Eleazar Williams. Erected by the Jean Nicolet chapter, Daughters of the American Revolution, 1926.

French government. Eleazar signed the abdication papers but later changed his mind and claimed his rightful ascendancy to the French throne as Louis XVII. The Prince of Joinville denied Eleazar's rendition of the tale, and Eleazar was denied his claim to royalty. He later married the daughter of a French-Canadian blacksmith and settled in a log cabin near DePere, Wisconsin.

The Reverend Eleazar Williams' story first gained popularity through an 1853 book entitled *The Lost Prince*, by John H. Hanson. Later the Reverend's tale was adapted into a best-selling novel titled *Lazarre*, by Mary Hartwell Catherwood. Although Williams was considered an impostor in France, his claim was believed by several Wisconsonites, including the Wisconsin Conservation Division, which dedicated a state park to him named Lost Dauphin State Park at his home site, south of DePere, Wisconsin. The Wisconsin Historical Society declared the site a national landmark and put up an official marker. The plaque states that the Reverend Eleazar Williams, the missing dauphin of France, Louis XVII, lived there.

The Resurrected Princess

> Tell Sverdlov that the entire family has met the same fate as its head.

This coded telegram was delivered on the morning of July 17, 1918, to the Council of People's Commissars in Moscow from a government official in Siberia. The message referred to an event that occurred only a few hours earlier in Ekaterinburg, a Siberian mining town now known as Sverdlosvk. . . .

Before dawn on the morning of July 17, 1918, the Russian Czar Nicholas II, his German-born wife, Empress Alexandra, their five children, personal servants, and physician were ordered by Bolshevik soldiers of the Communist revolutionary government to prepare for evacuation from their home in Ekaterinburg, where they had been held prisoners in exile. The soldiers then forced the royal family into the cellar to await further instructions. Frightened and cold in their damp, underground prison, they huddled close together in a corner of the tiny room.

All at once the cellar door burst open, and the soldiers sprayed the family with machine gun fire. To make sure that all were dead, the Bolsheviks stabbed them with bayonets and rifle butts. Then, they carted the bodies to an empty mine shaft, where they poured acid on the bodies, set them on fire, and then dumped the disfigured corpses down the shaft.

After this final, brutal act, authenticated history of the last Romanov czar and his family ends. Two years later, however, Act Two of that gruesome murder begins, with the "resurrection" of Anastasia, youngest daughter of Nicholas II.

In 1920, a woman calling herself Anna Anderson tried to commit suicide by jumping into a canal in Berlin, Germany. Rescued by police, she was committed at her own request to Daldorf Asylum, a mental institution. Although doctors judged her perfectly sane, she spent the next two years there, refusing to reveal her identity. Finally, trusting one of the nurses who promised her she would not be sent back to Russia, Anna Anderson confessed that she was Anastasia, only surviving daughter of Czar Nicholas II, and therefore heir to the Romanov estates and fortunes.

The alleged Anastasia said she survived the mass slaughter of her family by hiding under the dead body of one of her sisters. Two anti-Bolshevik soldiers, brothers named Chaivosky, noticed life in her body. While the other soldiers slept awhile after carting the bodies to the mine, the Chaivosky brothers smuggled seventeen-year-old Anastasia out of Russia and into Rumania. According to Anna, she married one of the brothers and had a son.

When her husband was killed by Bolsheviks who had learned of his rescuing the czar's daughter, Anna left the child in an orphanage and soon lost track of his whereabouts. Alone and destitute, Anna then traveled to Berlin in search of relatives, where she eventually tried to commit suicide.

The nurse had heard stories about one of the czar's family having survived the assassination from former German prisoners of war captured by Russians in World War I. Although many alleged Anastasias had previously come forth, they had all been disowned by the Romanov family as impostors. In order to verify Anna Anderson's claim, the nurse asked several relatives of the real Anastasia and a few former employees of the czar to visit the woman claiming to be Anastasia. Anna Anderson identified each person as they entered her hospital room, including Princess Xenia, Anastasia's second cousin, the Romanov children's former nurse, Sascha, and Gleb Blotkin, their childhood playmate and son of Nicholas' personal physician. Then Anna correctly identified photographs and heirlooms of the Romanov family.

The relatives and employees admitted Anna bore the same physical traits of the genuine Anastasia, most noticeably a protruding bone in her left foot. One of the czar's former physicians found her body riddled with bullet and bayonet scars, particularly on her chin. The physical evidence convinced the physician that Anna was the true grand duchess, Anastasia. The others concurred, and on the basis of their testimony, the alleged Anastasia was released from the Asylum in 1922.

When the public read the news, disbelievers in Anna Anderson's story pointed out there was no death certificate for Chaivosky, nor any orphanage records for her son. They doubted she could have traveled from Rumania to Berlin by herself without a passport or money. Skeptics further questioned why the presumed Anastasia refused to speak either Russian or English. Moreover, a German journalist discovered that Franziska Schanzkowski, a Polish girl, disappeared from a Berlin boarding house shortly before the alleged Anastasia was rescued from the Berlin canal. The journalist suggested Anna and Franziska were the same girl. Although many distant relatives of Anastasia's family championed her cause, the German House of Hesse, her mother Alexandra's side of the family, refused to accept the woman as the grand duchess, wanting to insure themselves a prior right to the Romanov inheritance.

In 1928, the alleged Anastasia made her debut into American society when Princess Xenia, now Mrs. W. B. Leeds of Philadelphia, invited her to stay at her home on Long Island, New York, and sent her the passage money.

Sometime during the middle of the 1930s Anastasia left Princess Xenia's and dropped out of sight. Some people presumed her dead. Then in 1941, she resurfaced and brought suit against the House of Hesse to gain her legacy. The suit dragged on and was never settled. By 1950, Anna Anderson, the name she now used exclusively, was back in Germany, destitute, and living in a shack on the edge of the Black Forest.

Several biographies of the grand duchess were published around this time, as well as a play entitled *Anastasia*. Upon learning of the literary works about her life, Anna Anderson protested the works' being published without her knowledge or consent. The play's producers solved the problem by sending Anna a script to assure her she was not being libeled, and the biographers gave her a share of their royalties.

In 1957, playwright Guy Bolton adapted the play into English for Broadway. After meeting the woman claiming to be Anastasia, he said, "I am prepared to stick my neck out on the side of the believers." The play then was made into a motion picture, from which Anna received at least twelve thousand dollars in royalties. Thus the presumed royal princess was finally relieved of an impoverished life.

Then in February, 1957, Anna Anderson's thirty-seven-year fight for her claimed identity seemed to be settled. The Eighty-Third Civil Chamber of the West Berlin District Court weighed the testimony of four anthropologists who compared the confor-

Is this woman this little girl? The real Anastasia is shown here near a tennis court in 1909, next to a photo of Anna Anderson, before her court appearance to claim her identity, and the Romanov inheritance, in 1981.

mations of Anna's ears, nose, and cheeks to photographs of the real teenaged Anastasia. Key testimony in the case was presented by a former World War I Austrian prisoner of war in Russia, Hans Joachim Mayer, who joined the Bolsheviks in 1918. According to Mayer, he witnessed the Ekaterinburg executions and saw Anastasia's dead body after the massacre. Following Mayer's testimony, the judges announced that, in their opinion, the woman Anna Anderson was not the Romanov Princess Anastasia and had no claim to any part of the late czar's estate. The judges decreed that Nicholas II's foreign holdings go to the German ducal House of Hesse.

For the rest of her life, Anna Anderson never stopped believing herself Grand Duchess Anastasia. She appealed the West Berlin verdict until 1970, when the court, unable to confirm or refute her claim, closed the case for good. She eventually married John E. Manahan, an historian from Charlottesville, Virginia.

On February 12, 1984, Anna's sixty-five-year fight for her identity finally ended, as Anna Anderson Manahan, alleged Grand Duchess Anastasia Nikolaevna Romanov, last member of the imperial Romanovs of Russia, succumbed to pneumonia in Charlottesville, Virginia, and died at the age of eighty-two.

The Pretender to Marriage

Arnaud du Tilb, a Frenchman who lived in the 1540s, possessed an uncanny ability to mimic others. He could watch someone for a minute, then perfectly imitate that person's expressions, mannerisms, and speech. He used his talent to gain himself a wife.

One day Arnaud was resting in a thicket near a pond, when a beautiful woman strolled into the hollow. Not realizing she was being observed, the woman disrobed and went for a swim in the pond. Du Tilb was struck by her beauty and eventually learned that her name was Bertrande. She was married to Martin

Guerre and had a son. Martin was a scoundrel, and he frequently quarreled with Bertrande and her father, who accused Martin of wanting him to die so he could claim Bertrande's inheritance.

Not long afterwards, Martin Guerre, tired of his father-in-law's accusations, left his wife and son and disappeared. When Martin Guerre ran away, Arnaud was traveling across France. One day he encountered Martin, who was in the Spanish army. Arnaud pretended to become Guerre's close friend, and the runaway husband told du Tilb his life story.

After learning Guerre's history and studying his mannerisms and speech, Arnaud returned to Guerre's village, Artigues, and began his imposture as the prodigal husband Martin. He duped not only Bertrande, but both their families as well. Arnaud and Bertrande lived happily together for three years, and she bore him two daughters.

Du Tilb's imposture might have continued forever, if a stranger who knew the real Martin Guerre had not stopped in Artigues. The stranger said he had seen Martin Guerre eighteen months before in a distant French province. Martin, who had lost a leg in the battle of St. Quinten, had told the man he did not intend to go home while his father-in-law lived.

Bertrande's family now recalled small incidences, unnoticed before, that made them suspect du Tilb was an impostor. For instance, he was not as quarrelsome as the Martin Guerre they remembered, and his speech was different from the known Guerre's, who was a Biscayan and spoke in a mixture of Spanish, French, and Gascon. Bertrande refused to believe the man was not her real husband. The family divided into factions, finally bringing the case to court.

During the trial, a stream of people testified in Arnaud's behalf. Thirty-seven other witnesses swore the man was not Martin Guerre. Some stressed the physical differences between the two men. Guerre's nose was flatter, and he was thinner and taller than the man in the defendant's box. The shoemaker who had made Guerre's shoes stated this man's foot was larger than Martin Guerre's. Furthermore, Guerre was an excellent wrestler and fencer, yet the defendant knew nothing about these sports. Then almost a dozen people who knew Arnaud du Tilb swore that the defendant was one and the same. The judge gave his verdict: guilty as charged. Arnaud du Tilb was sentenced to death.

Du Tilb appealed to the Parliament of Toulouse, which ordered a search to locate the real Martin Guerre. Several months later, the true roving husband was found and brought secretly to the appeals court at Toulouse. He made a surprise entrance into the courtroom. Du Tilb, an excellent actor, calmly said, "This man is either mad or an impostor." An observer later wrote, "At that moment, Guerre seemed the impostor, and the prisoner a wronged man."

The crucial moment of the trial occurred when Bertrande and Guerre's four sisters saw Martin. The moment his oldest sister saw him, she cried, "Oh my brother, Martin Guerre." Bertrande ran to her husband and asked forgiveness for believing in du Tilb and declared she wished the impostor dead. The real Martin Guerre replied, "A wife always has ways, unknown to every other living soul, of knowing a husband. It is impossible that a woman can have been imposed upon if she had not entertained a secret wish to be unfaithful."

The judge admonished Guerre that a husband who leaves a beautiful woman to waste her best years alone deserves some punishment. Then the judge pronounced du Tilb guilty of fraud and condemned him to make the *amende honorable*, in which the guilty person, with bare head and feet, a halter around his neck, and a lighted torch in his hand, asks pardon of God, the king, the nation, and the family he has wronged. After du Tilb made his penance in the marketplace, he was taken outside Martin Guerre's house and hanged.

Several books have been written about the husband impostor, including one published in 1561 by the judge in the case,

Jean de Coras. In 1983, the latest renditions of the husband impostor appeared: one a book titled *The Return of Martin Guerre*, by Natalie Zemon Davis; and the other a motion picture with the same name.

The fact that a stranger could convince a woman he was her husband for that long is considered so amazing in the annals of hoaxes that several experts believe Bertrande knew all along that the man claiming to be Martin Guerre was not her husband. However, as she was not free to remarry until her wandering husband's whereabouts or death had been ascertained, and finding herself alone with a child to raise, she either subtly or explicitly conspired in the imposture. Only when du Tilb was on the brink of unmasking, and consequently tarnishing her honor, did Bertrande take action against the fake Martin Guerre.

The Great Impostor

Newsweek magazine called him "the Persistent Phony," and *Time* judged him a "Superior Sort of Liar." It was the author Robert Crichton who gave him the nickname that stuck when he wrote his book *The Great Impostor* in the late 1950s. While most impostors play the role of only one other person, the Great Impostor played many parts, performing each as if he had trained all his life to become the doctor, lawyer, or other professional he was impersonating. Asked why he spent his life duping people into believing he was someone else, he said, "Being an impostor is a tough habit to break."

The hoaxer's real name is Ferdinand Waldo Demara, Jr. One winter day the teenage Ferdinand found a woman's mannequin legs in a trash can. He partially buried them in a snowdrift on the side of the street, then hid where he could watch what happened. Motorists passing by skidded to a stop and leaped out of their cars to help the "poor buried woman." When they discovered the legs were artificial, they went on their way, and

Ferdinand Waldo Demara, Jr., "The Great Impostor", in 1952.

Ferdinand came out of his hiding place to pull the prank all over again. Ferdinand Demara, Jr., has been pulling pranks ever since.

Ferdinand, whom most people called Fred, was born in 1921 in Lawrence, Massachusetts, the son of a wealthy movie theater owner. When Fred was twelve, his father suddenly went bankrupt. Fred hated living in poverty so much that for the rest of his life he sought to become a man of money and respectability. Some people suggest that Demara's quest to reenter high society and wealth was the reason he always impersonated professionals.

When he was sixteen, Ferdinand ran away from home and joined a Cistercian monastery, an order of farm workers in Valley Falls, Rhode Island. After a year, the abbot suggested that teaching was a more suitable career for Fred, and he transferred to another monastery, the Brothers of Christian Charity. He stayed with the Brothers for three years, then enlisted in the army. He went AWOL almost immediately and a week later enlisted in the U.S. navy. The navy sent Demara to hospital school at Norfolk, Virginia. "That was my first taste of medicine," he later commented. Norfolk was also his first attempt at imposture. In order to apply for Officer Candidate School, Demara faked a college background from Iowa State College and a letter of reference from Senator Capper of Kansas. However, Ferdinand failed to include enough mathematics courses in his phony transcript and his application was rejected. He promptly deserted the navy.

At this time, Demara joined an order of Trappist monks near Louisville, Kentucky. He presented himself as Robert L. French, a graduate of the University of Michigan, with a Ph.D. in psychology from Stanford, and a Sterling Research Fellowship at Yale. Ferdinand had obtained French's background by reading a college catalogue where French had served on the faculty. This technique worked so well that Demara used college catalogues from then on as his main reference when choosing someone to impersonate. Still masquerading as French, Demara soon left the Trappists and joined an order of Catholic teachers, where he studied scholastic philosophy and ethics at De Paul University. His records show he made straight A's. "Maybe the instructors were impressed by my Ph.D.," Demara said.

Sometimes circumstances forced Demara to change roles. "In this little game I was playing, there always comes a time when you find yourself getting in too deep. You've made good friends who believe in you, and you don't want them to get hurt and disillusioned. You begin to worry about what they'll think if somebody exposes you as a phony."

One of those times occurred when Demara faced ordination as a priest. "I thought at the time that I had a true religious vocation," Demara later said. "But I couldn't go ahead without telling those men the truth about myself. So I disappeared."

He reappeared a year later, first as a psychology teacher at Gannon College in Erie, Pennsylvania, then in Los Angeles,

California, as an orderly at a sanitarium, and next in Washington, where, posing as Dr. French again, he landed a position as a psychology instructor at St. Martin's College near Olympia. In Washington, he was popular and made many influential friends. The sheriff made him a deputy to enforce laws around the college campus.

Demara said that in Washington he felt safe for the first time since he deserted the navy and would have settled there permanently if his luck had held. But fate seemed to have declared that Ferdinand Waldo Demara, Jr., was to be a wanderer, for two FBI agents found him in Washington, where they issued a warrant for his arrest for desertion of the navy.

At his court-martial, Demara was found guilty and sentenced to one and a half years in the U.S. Disciplinary Barracks at San Pedro, California. During his prison term, the army also caught up with Ferdinand and discharged him. When he was released from prison, he scoured his college catalogues and decided to assume the identity of Dr. Cecil B. Hamann, a biologist on the faculty of a college in Wilmore, Kentucky. To learn more about the eminent doctor, Demara managed to obtain Hamann's college records and birth certificate. Demara then secured a teaching position in a parochial school through joining the Christian Brothers of Instruction in Alfred, Maine.

When the newspapers published a story about the brilliant Dr. Hamann, a former student of the real doctor read the article and sent him a copy. Hamann vowed to take action but surprisingly never got around to doing anything at all. Demara had another close call when he was attending an educational convention in Chicago. As he stood in line at the registration desk of his hotel, a man behind him asked the desk clerk if there was any mail for Cecil B. Hamann. The encounter gave Demara quite a jolt, but he stayed put, realizing that Dr. Hamann had never seen his impersonator. So for the convention, Demara registered as Brother John, his religious name.

When the Brothers sent "Dr. Hamann" to Grand Falls, New

Brunswick, to study theology in preparation for his solemn vows, Demara became fascinated with the study of medicine and spent hours talking to a Dr. Joseph C. Cyr, a general practitioner recently graduated from medical school at Quebec's Laval University. Demara told Cyr that he had been a physician before joining the Brothers. Once, when Dr. Cyr was treating another Brother for rheumatoid arthritis, he asked Demara for his opinion. "Dr. Hamann" suggested bee venom, which he had read about in a medical journal. The treatment worked, and from then on, Dr. Cyr's admiration for "Hamann" grew by leaps and bounds. When Cyr asked Demara's help in obtaining a medical license in Maine so he could practice medicine in the United States, Demara took his credentials to Maine on the presumption that he would give them to the medical board there. However, Demara claimed he became so busy he forgot to deliver Cyr's records to the board. Demara's next imposture was as Dr. Joseph C. Cyr.

Demara left the Christian Brothers, not wanting to become an ordained brother. During the Korean War, he joined the Royal Canadian Navy posing as Dr. Cyr. He was given the rank of Lieutenant-Surgeon and assigned the post of medical officer aboard the destroyer *Cayuga*. Demara used both his medical training in the navy and the experience he gained from working in the hospital sanitarium to give him confidence to perform minor operations such as pulling teeth, removing tonsils, or treating colds.

His first major operation involved operating on a wounded Korean soldier who had received a bullet wound barely an inch from his heart. Using the captain's cabin as an operating room, Demara later confessed, "I kept one basic principle in my mind. The less cutting you do, the less patching up you have to do afterwards."

His next case involved even more complicated surgery. Demara successfully performed a lung resection (lung removal) on a Korean soldier who had been shot with a dumdum bullet that had destroyed most of his right lung. Demara made the incision but ran into trouble when the clippers used to cut ribs were found missing. Demara improvised by using an amputation saw and sawing the ribs. When later Demara went ashore to check on his patient, the soldier was fine, but Demara was shocked by the primitive medical care given the South Korean troops. He obtained permission to go ashore daily and treat these casualties. Unknown to Demara, the public relations officer aboard the *Cayuga* released a story to the press about the courageous surgery being performed by Dr. Cyr. This time the real Dr. Joseph Cyr read the article and took action. Cyr exposed Demara as an impostor, and the Royal Navy brought him back from Korea to the United States, where he was questioned by a board of surgeons and dismissed for giving fraudulent medical treatment.

Even after the exposure of his fraud, many people continued to believe in Demara. A nineteen-year-old mother in Detroit, Michigan, asked him to perform a lung operation on her infant daughter, and a lumber camp in British Columbia offered to hire him as their doctor with no questions asked. In addition, the *Cayuga*'s officers praised his medical skill, his humane care of patients, and his untiring medical services on their own behalf.

In 1952, Ferdinand Demara posed as Martin Godgart (a real teacher from Connecticut) and taught French, Latin, and English in North Haven, Maine. He was a popular member of the small island town and led a sea scout troop, taught Sunday School at the Baptist Church, and portrayed Santa Claus for the town's children. Then, for an unknown reason, he showed friends a picture, without the caption, that *Life* magazine had printed of him. Curious, the townspeople checked on him, and his best friend there sent his fingerprints (lifted from a beer can) to the police. Demara was given a suspended sentence since he had done no harm.

"I don't know what I'm going to do next," he told *Life's*

reporters, who printed his complete story in their January 28, 1952, issue.

Then the Great Impostor disappeared, presumably to embark upon another masquerade.

With all the hard work involved in being a successful impostor, one wonders why anyone would go to all that trouble. For example, why would people with the intelligence of Demara, or the wit and cunning of Sarah Wilson, spend their lives trying to be other people, when it would seem that with their ability they could have been successful adults just by being themselves?

Many reasons motivate impostors including fame, wealth, or regal titles. Sometimes they want to hide something in their past, such as having committed a crime. Other impostors, no matter how intelligent or capable they are, do not like themselves. These people prefer to go through life being someone else, who they imagine lives in better circumstances. Whatever the impostors' motives, they all enjoy the challenge of putting on masks of deception and trying to fool others.

CHAPTER SEVEN

ART HOAXES

In July, 1984, in the small town of Livorno, Italy, a crowd of art experts and townspeople watched eagerly as dredgers began sifting through seven feet of mud at the bottom of a junk-strewn canal known locally as the royal ditch. The goal of the dredgers was to recover the long-lost stone sculptures of the locally born artist Amedeo Modigliani. Should the sculptures be discovered, they would crown the Modigliani exhibit being mounted in the town's Progressive Museum of Contemporary Art to celebrate the one hundredth anniversary of the artist's birth.

Most people know Modigliani by his colorful paintings of languid women with elongated necks, which, when painted at the beginning of this century, were hallmarks of modern art. Yet, Modigliani's first love was originally sculpture. Today, only twenty-six of his sculptures exist. Rumor has it that one day, about seventy-five years ago, after his friends had rudely criticized his work, Modigliani exploded in a fit of anger. He gathered up all the sculptures in his studio and tossed them into the nearby canal, where they sank to the bottom. In the years that followed he made a few more sculptures, but ill health forced him to turn to painting, which was a less strenuous activity. He died in 1920, at the age of thirty-five. Ever since, art historians have dreamed of discovering the lost Modiglianis.

As the dredging machines dipped their rubber-tipped claws into the muck at the bottom of the canal, they began to unearth an assortment of junk—several guns, a rocking horse, bicycles, and even a complete set of bathroom fittings. A week went by without revealing any lost pieces of art. Then, at nine in the morning on July 24, 1984, the first sculpture was found. Later that day, a second was dredged up, and then a third was found two weeks later on August 9. For students of Modigliani's work, these sculptures were the find of the century. Each carving was of a face, about twice life-size and displayed the characteristic long nose and stylized features. Art experts rushed to Livorno and declared the pieces "very important and certainly Modiglianis." The sculptures, subsequently named Modi 1, 2, and 3, were promptly disinfected, cleaned, and added to the exhibit in the museum.

Unfortunately, the euphoria did not last long. Six weeks later, three university students confessed that they had carved Modi 2, copying it from a photograph in the museum catalogue. The students said that they had just been playing a prank. The boys had known about the dredging and said to themselves, "Why not help them to find something?" They added, "It's not our fault that so many people made a mistake." To dispel criticism, they even demonstrated how they had created the sculpture on a three-hour television special. Then in September, the creator of Modi 1 and 3 stepped forward. He was a dockworker and former art student who claimed he wanted "to reveal the false values of art critics and mass media."

Art critics later admitted that they had been so eager to discover the lost Modiglianis that they had jumped to their conclusions too hastily. One consolation derived from the publicity was that a record number of visitors came to the museum to view the Modigliani centenary exhibit, and the museum and city earned a thirty-five-thousand-dollar profit over the cost of the dredging. But perhaps, if the original rumor is true, the genuine sculptures are still waiting to be discovered someday, deep in the mud of the royal ditch.

Copying works by well-known artists has occurred for centuries. The ancient Romans copied Greek sculpture because they admired the Greek style. Like students of literature, art students have traditionally copied works of the masters in order to learn new techniques. The question of forgery begins when the copier tries to pass off his or her own work as that of the original artist. Nearly every kind of artwork with monetary value has been forged at some time, including furniture, carpets, ivory carvings, silverware, stamps, jewelry, etchings, drawings, sculptures and paintings.

A lavishly decorated gold cup shaped like a seashell balanced on the back of a bejewelled dragon is one of the most beautiful treasures at the Metropolitan Museum of Art in New York. For many years it was thought to have been made by the great sixteenth-century Italian goldsmith, Benvenuto Cellini. The art world was shocked when, in January, 1984, the museum announced that both the gold cup and forty-four other works in its collection were fakes, all made by a German master craftsman of the nineteenth century named Reinhold Vasters. Not only had one of the museum curators discovered the working drawings for Vasters' creations, but careful examination of the cup revealed that it had been put together with solder in a way not known in the Renaissance.

The seventeenth-century Flemish artist, Anthony Van Dyck, painted about seventy pictures in his lifetime. Yet nearly two thousand paintings in museums and private collections around the world have been attributed to him. Clearly most of these have been forged. Of the nineteenth-century French landscape painter, Jean-Baptiste Camille Corot, experts have said that of the three thousand pictures he painted, eight thousand are in the United States and England. As long as there is a demand for paintings by well-loved artists, forgers seem happy to provide them.

Salvador Dali, leader of the Surrealist movement in art, has a reputation that results as much from his bizarre life style and curly mustaches, as from his creation of fantastic paintings. As a young artist in the 1930s he impressed the art world and the public with his dripping clocks and dream-like landscapes and quickly became very rich. Now ill and in his nineties, he no longer paints and lives in seclusion in his house in Figueras, Spain, while, in the outside world, unscrupulous dealers make millions in fake Dali prints.

In the last few years millions of dollars worth of fake Dali lithographs have been sold in the United States alone. Some of these are photographic reproductions with false signatures, while others are drawings done by other artists on sheets of paper signed by Dali. In February, 1986, a New York County grand jury indicted seven people for selling fake Dali prints. Customers had been sold photographic reproductions, actually worth about ten dollars each, for three thousand dollars each.

One source of the counterfeit problem is Dali's habit of signing blank sheets of paper on which artisans would supposedly, later, print lithographs from his plates. It is said that assistants used to stand on either side, passing sheets of paper to him as fast as he could sign his name. Although Dali stopped this practice in 1980, in his lifetime he has signed approximately 350,000 such sheets. It is not known how many of these sheets have been stolen.

Dali himself has been no help in fighting the counterfeiters. Part of this is because he is reluctant to become involved in any legal action against the art dealers; part is because he is ill; part is because of his distrust of the courts; but, as much as anything else, it is due to his pride over being faked. Art collectors need to resolve this problem, but without Dali's help, it will take experts years to sort out the genuine Dalis from the fakes.

Imitation is supposed to be the sincerest form of flattery, yet when imitation begins to be represented as the original, it creates problems for museums, collectors, art dealers and scholars. Art forgery is illegal for a number of reasons. To begin with, to perpetrate an object falsely is an outright lie. Secondly, collectors buy art as an investment and expect to be able to resell their purchases for as much as or more than they originally paid. If their art proves to be a fake, then its value plummets. Thirdly, art historians study art to learn about the artist and his or her techniques. False informaton from a fake gives an inaccurate view of the artist. And perhaps most important is the fact that artists themselves are cheated when their work is forged, especially if the imitated art is inferior or reflects a point of view not held by the artist.

Detecting Forgeries

Occasionally museums or art galleries mount exhibits of forgeries, which are both instructive and entertaining. By looking at two pieces of art placed side by side—one forged, the other real—the qualities that make fine art can be appreciated better. In the words of one writer, "The forger has sharpened our aesthetic sensibilities, has made us draw the fine line between our elusive aspiration—the absolute truth of a work of art—and our much too easy ideal—what each period thinks a classic work of the past *ought* to look like."

When, for instance, a fake Impressionist painting is compared to a real painting by an artist such as Monet, Cézanne, or Seurat, the fake is obviously different. Whereas the paintings of the real French Impressionists are distinguished by their clear tones, fine gradations of values (lights and darks), and clearly drawn forms, the fakes frequently show dirty colors, a lack of a sense of values, and often the forms in them are either unrecognizable or indistinct.

To the trained eye, a fake piece of art stands out from the genuine because it fails to reproduce the artist's vision and technique. Only a few people, however, possess the ability to detect a forgery just by looking at it, and even then, their opinions are subjective. Today, a large arsenal of scientific tests aids the art detective in obtaining incontrovertible evidence to judge an object false or genuine.

The Pierpont Morgan Library in New York City recently used one such technique, called neutron autoradiography, to verify that an illustration in a supposedly medieval manuscript, long suspected to be false, was indeed a forgery. First a medical research reactor was used to expose the painting to a beam of electrons. Then a series of x-ray films was placed over the work. The radiation from the decay of chemicals on the page would then expose the x-ray plate in much the same way that a photographic plate is exposed to light. Because the radioactive atoms of different chemicals decay at different rates, the pattern of exposure on the plates would indicate the nature of the chemical. As a result, the Pierpont Library discovered that one of the pigments in the "medieval" manuscript contained a material, copper arsenite, which had only been used between 1778 and 1814, long after medieval times. Thus, the curators confirmed what they already suspected—that this beautiful manuscript illustration was the work of a nineteenth-century artist known as the Spanish Forger. Although the identity of the Spanish Forger (so named because his work was once attributed to an English painter living in Spain) is unknown, he is now credited with at least forty-six forgeries of medieval and early Renaissance paintings.

For oil paintings, routine chemical analysis of small samples of paint can reveal their composition. If a paint contains a chemical that is newer than the painting purports to be, then the painting is likely to be a forgery. Other methods of determining the age of paint include looking at it with an electron microbeam probe, using a nuclear reactor to bombard the painting with low energy thermal neutrons, and heating the pigments to high temperatures, and then examining the light that they emit.

To reveal a sketch hidden below the surface of a painting, infrared photography, reflectography, and neutron autoradiography can be used. Frequently artists paint their pictures on top of old canvases, so that, in some cases, there is a buildup of many paintings. Ordinary x-rays can reveal these underpaintings. If the underpainting is newer than the painting on top claims to be, then it signals a forgery.

Three of the most successful art forgers of the twentieth century are Han van Meegeren, Alceo Dossena, and David Stein. All successfully fooled the experts for a long period of time, and all, except Dossena, who was cheated by his unscrupulous agents, earned large sums of money for their work.

Han van Meegeren

During World War II, many Nazi officers confiscated valuable works of art. One of these, a painting called *The Adulteress* by the Dutch master Vermeer, had been purchased by Air Marshal Hermann Goering. After the war, the Allied Art Commission worked to restore works such as the Vermeer to their rightful owners. When *The Adulteress* was traced back to the Dutchman Han van Meegeren, he was arrested as a collaborator and put in jail, for it was a crime to have traded with the enemy.

At first van Meegeren refused to tell how he obtained the painting, claiming that it had originally belonged to an old Italian family whose name must be kept secret. Finally, after six weeks in jail and with no hope of release, van Meegeren decided to tell the truth. He had painted the picture himself!

Dutch artist, Han van Meegeren in the defendant box. His painting, "Isaac Blesses Jacob" is shown on the wall.

Not only that, he confessed to having painted several other Vermeers that then hung in national museums and important collections.

Needless to say, no one believed van Meegeren at first. The pictures were so good that experts had never even suspected they might be forgeries. No one wanted to believe they were forged, for then a lot of art experts would look extremely foolish.

Finally, a test was devised to prove once and for all whether or not van Meegeren was capable of painting a Vermeer. The police agreed to provide him with a studio and the materials he needed to make a new painting in the same style. "Show us," they challenged him, "that you can paint like Vermeer." Then, under the constant supervision of two policemen, van Meegeren began his new painting, *Young Christ Teaching in the Temple*. When he finished, it was even better than some of his earlier forgeries. The public was impressed, and the charge of collaboration was dropped. Extensive newspaper coverage made van Meegeren famous, and everyone was eager to know how he had developed his expert technique.

Han van Meegeren grew up in the small town of Deventer, Holland, where his father was a school teacher. By the age of nine, in the year 1893, young Han had developed a passion for drawing and entertained himself by creating, through drawings, an imaginary world of kings and lions. In high school, Han's art teacher, Bartus Korteling, recognized his art talent and encouraged him. Korteling's tastes were old-fashioned, and he preferred art work in the style of Dutch masters such as Rembrandt, Vermeer, and Frans Hals. Guided by Korteling, van Meegeren began to paint in the manner of these seventeenth-century artists. He also learned to grind pigments and manufacture his own paints, just as the old masters had done.

After high school, Han went to an architectural school, where he spent most of his time studying painting rather than architecture, and as a result, failed his exams. However, in 1913, he won a gold medal for a watercolor painting he entered in a competition given by The Hague Academy. The watercolor was painted in the style of the seventeenth-century masters he loved so well. Subsequently, he attended the Academy and received a degree in art. For a few years, Han van Meegeren worked as a painter, had successful gallery shows, and sold his work. By 1930 however, his art career, still rooted in the old-fashioned style, appeared to be at an end.

At this point, an art critic for a local newspaper approached Han van Meegeren and offered to write a positive review of his work, if van Meegeren would pay him. Van Meegeren was furious and became convinced that all art critics were unscrupulous. Shortly thereafter, a friend of van Meegeren found a genuine Frans Hals painting in a junk shop and showed it to a well-known expert, Dr. Abraham Bredius. Mistakenly, Bredius pronounced the picture a fake. These two incidents planted the seeds that would eventually grow into van Meegeren's magnificent forgeries. Believing all art experts to be fools as well, van Meegeren decided to get his revenge on them by painting a fake Vermeer, and when the work had been hung in a museum, announcing that he had painted it himself.

Thus began four years of hard work. To guarantee that the canvas he used was of the appropriate age (van Meegeren knew that laboratory tests would quickly reveal a piece of modern canvas), he bought an inexpensive seventeenth-century painting and then carefully removed all the paint. Next he researched the exact ingredients Vermeer had used to make his paints. He mixed them together as he had learned from his high school art teacher. Van Meegeren then made paint brushes from badger hair (which he extracted from shaving brushes) because he knew that these were the kind of brushes available in Vermeer's time.

Van Meegeren's biggest problem was making the painting look as if it were three-hundred-years old. Normally in such an old picture the paint would be dry and hard, for it takes many years for oil paint to completely dry. Also, the picture would be impregnated with tiny hairline cracks. Through extensive research, van Meegeren discovered two oils that dried quickly. He also found that by carefully baking his paintings he could get the paint to be just the right hardness. To create cracks, van Meegeren worked out an ingenious method which involved painting his picture over another that already had cracks. In the baking process, these cracks would emerge in the new painting. For a final touch, van Meegeren brushed the surface of the painting with India ink. As he removed the ink from the painting, some of it remained in the cracks, giving the appearance of genuine ancient dust.

When all his preparations were complete, van Meegeren began work on his first paintings. Using four seventeenth-century canvases, he painted two fake Vermeers, one fake Frans Hals, and one in the manner of Ter Borch, another Dutch painter. These paintings all depicted scenes from everyday life and gave van Meegeren confidence in his own ability to produce a believable fake. When these practice paintings were finished, they looked convincingly genuine. Instead of trying to sell them, however, van Meegeren embarked upon a new, much larger and more ambitious painting, which he called *Christ at Emmaus*. It was a simple, strong composition of four figures grouped around a table, with a window on the left through which light played over the scene—a typical Vermeer device. When he finished, he signed the picture with Vermeer's name. Then, to give the appearance of three centuries worth of wear and tear, he tore the edges of the canvas and scraped off the paint in a few places. At last, in the spring of 1937, he was ready to sell the painting.

Now van Meegeren needed to get the painting authenticated by an expert. His first choice was Dr. Bredius, who by then was eighty-three years old. Through a friend, van Meegeren sent the art critic the painting. Dr. Bredius was so enchanted with the piece he kept it for two days, then gladly wrote a certificate that said, "This glorious work of Vermeer, the great Vermeer of Delft, has emerged—thank God!—from the darkness where it lay for many years undefiled and just as it left the artist's studio." He then wrote an article for an art magazine in which he praised the painting. The Boymans Museum in Holland became interested in the painting, and through a group of benefactors, bought it for the equivalent of about a quarter of a million dollars.

At this point, instead of announcing that he was the real Vermeer artist and had succeeded in fooling the art establishment as originally planned, van Meegeren wildly spent his money and began planning a new painting. He called this work *Interior With Drinkers* and painted it in the style of Pieter de Hooch. This painting as well as the next, a fake Vermeer called *The Last Supper,* was sold to a wealthy shipowner. Between 1939 and 1943 van Meegeren painted and sold five more Vermeers, including one to the famous Rijksmuseum in Amsterdam.

It was only after the war ended that van Meegeren's world began to fall apart. By then he had divorced his wife and become dependent upon alcohol and drugs. Although he had survived the accusation of Nazi collaboration, in October, 1947, van Meegeren was tried for fraud and found guilty. His health grew increasingly worse, and in December of that year, he died. Ironically, the value of his early paintings, signed with his own name and which he could not sell in his lifetime, have risen in value since then. In 1976, an original van Meegeren sold in London for four hundred and fifty dollars.

Nevertheless, the real achievement of Han van Meegeren lies in the perfection of his imitation of the old Master technique. He will long be remembered as the master forger of this century.

Alceo Dossena, Sculptor of the Ages

In 1920, Alceo Dossena, an Italian stonecutter who had studied the works of Renaissance masters such as Michelangelo, began carving his own versions of Renaissance sculpture. Dossena's skill was enormous, and his finished works appeared uncannily like real Michelangelo pieces. Soon his studio was filled with his works, all done in the style of old craftsmen.

Dossena was born in 1878, in Cremona, Italy, and started drawing at an early age. As a young man, he was apprenticed to a marble mason, and he learned how to repair damaged columns and stairways in old Italian churches and palaces. Later, Dossena learned to repair old sculptures and tombstones. The challenge of such work was to master the style of the original artist so well that the repair could not be detected.

Dossena was an excellent student and traveled extensively to do his work. In some cases, when a statue was too badly damaged to be repaired, Dossena would carve a new one. After carving it, he would artificially age the sculpture so that it would match its setting.

On Christmas Eve, 1916, Alceo Dossena was desperately in need of money to buy presents for his family. It was the middle of World War I, and he was in an army unit stationed in Rome. Dossena decided to try selling a stone madonna he had carved and aged to look antique. He took the statue to a cafe owner he knew. Although the man did not want the statue, he had a friend who did, a jeweler named Alberto Fasoli. Dossena could hardly believe his good fortune when Fasoli bought the madonna for one hundred lire!

Fasoli soon realized that the madonna was not old at all, but rather a skillful imitation, and he knew that if he could be fooled, so could others. If he could obtain more sculptures of the same sort, he could make a great deal of money. When Fasoli asked Dossena if he could supply him with more statues, Dossena gladly agreed.

After the war, Fasoli teamed up with an antique dealer named Romano Palesi. Together they set up a studio for Dossena in Rome and agreed to pay him a small monthly salary. As Dossena produced, they marketed the artwork worldwide. For nearly ten years Dossena happily sculpted for Fasoli and Palesi.

Fasoli and Palesi were a clever team. They were careful not to sell too many of the fake sculptures in the same place and thereby flood the market. They always concocted elaborate tales as to the source of each piece. Sometimes they even convinced respected art authorities to authenticate the sculpture, although in most cases they used dishonest experts who would authenticate a piece knowing it to be a fake.

Dossena's skill grew as he worked. Perhaps one of his greatest achievements was a pair of carved statues done in the style of Simone Martini, an early Renaissance painter. No one had known Martini to have sculpted, but Dossena's figures were so like those in Martini's *Annunciation* painting that the world was convinced they were genuine.

Unlike van Meegeren, who had focused on one historical period for his forgeries, Dossena's works ranged from classical, to the Middle Ages, and the Renaissance. Dossena was also versatile in his ability to work in different media. He was able to work equally well in bronze, wood, stone or clay. Although Dossena's sculptures were sold by his agents, who knew they were forgeries, Dossena himself never intended to fool anyone with his work. The Metropolitan Museum in New York, the Cleveland Museum in Ohio, and Boston's Museum of Fine Arts are among the many that were duped by Dossena's agents. Fasoli and Palesi made over two million dollars before their scheme was discovered. Of that they paid only thirty thousand to Dossena over a ten-year period. Dossena always believed that his works were being marketed as legitimate reproductions.

Dossena was meticulous in his efforts to achieve the correct effects of aging. For his Greek sculptures, he dipped the statues into a secret acid bath. For Gothic wood sculptures, which were often painted in many colors, Dossena used paint chipped off other carvings from the same period. However, even though Dossena carefully created the appropriate age *appearance* of his carvings, he was unconcerned whether or not they would fool experts. It was not his intention. Therefore, when adding wood to a seventeenth-century sculpture before converting it to one that would look as if it were carved in the thirteenth century, Dossena did not hesitate to use twentieth-century nails to hold the pieces together. When the sculpture, a madonna and child, was bought by the Cleveland Museum, an x-ray quickly revealed it to be phony.

Although other purchasers of Fasoli's antiques were beginning to suspect that the agent was a swindler, it was Dossena himself who revealed the scheme. When his wife died in 1927, Dossena was left with many unpaid bills. He went to Fasoli and asked him for money. Fasoli refused. Dossena decided to file a lawsuit. The ensuing publicity spread the news of Fasoli and Palesi's deception worldwide. Many art dealers and museums that had purchased Dossena's work at first refused to believe they were fakes, but eventually they were forced to admit they had been fooled. They all agreed, however, that Dossena was a great artist. Unfortunately, the value of his work was far less than that of an antique.

After the trial, Dossena continued to work, producing sculptures under his own name, and although the public eagerly went to his exhibits, few of his works sold. He died penniless in 1937.

David Stein, Master Forger of Modern Art

David Stein is only one of many pseudonyms used by this prolific forger of twentieth-century art. Also known as Philippe Ducrest, Georges Delauney, and Michel Honcourt, he produced thousands of art fakes during the 1960s. With amazing facility and speed, Stein produced masses of drawings in the style of many different modern artists. His skill was such that he could copy a Modigliani, Cocteau, Picasso, or Chagall with equal ease.

Unlike van Meegeren and Dossena, Stein had no need to make his work look old. He also did not have to worry that his works would be detected by his choice of paper or paint, for all the materials he needed were those currently available to any artist. On the other hand, David Stein's risk was in daring to imitate artists who were still alive. In the end this was his undoing.

Stein was found out when he sold some fake Chagall drawings to a dealer in New York. The dealer demanded the drawings be authenticated by a Chagall expert in France. Stein agreed and proceeded to have a fake authentication stamp made in New York. Then he stamped the backs of photographs of the drawings and returned them to the dealer. However, in his haste to make the sale, Stein had not allowed enough time for mail to travel to and from Paris, and thus tipped off the gallery owner that the drawings must be forgeries. When a police detective showed the drawings to Chagall, who happened to be in New York at the time, Chagall declared them "garbage."

In the end, David Stein was found guilty on ninety-seven counts of forgery. He was sentenced to three years in Sing Sing prison in New York state. While in prison, he continued to paint, and later fifty of his prison paintings sold in London for eleven thousand dollars. This time the paintings were signed with his own name.

Stein's wife wrote a book about his forgery career called *Three Picassos Before Breakfast*. The title was inspired by an incident in Italy when a dealer asked Stein if he had any Picassos to sell. Stein said he had some at his hotel and would bring them to the man the next day. By the time he returned to his hotel Stein was too tired to paint, so the next morning he got up very early and painted *seven* Picassos before breakfast. Today David Stein is out of prison and continues to paint.

Faked Lincoln Portraits

A lack of suitable photographs of a well-known person also provides the inspiration for forgers to create fakes. For instance, during his campaign and presidency, Abraham Lincoln had no

Abraham Lincoln's head on the body of John C. Calhoun.

THE FATHER, AND THE SAVIOUR OF OUR COUNTRY.

Entered according to Act of Congress, in the year 1865, by James F. Bodtker, in the Clerk's Office of the District Court of the United States for the District of Wisconsin.

Fake portrait of George Washington and Abraham Lincoln.

Faked portrait of Abraham Lincoln.

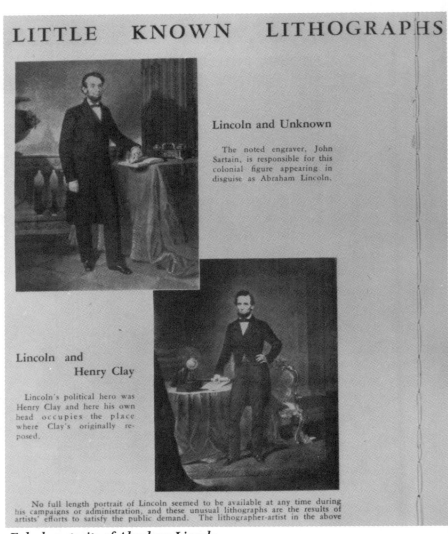

Lincoln and Unknown

The noted engraver, John Sartain, is responsible for this colonial figure appearing in disguise as Abraham Lincoln.

Lincoln and Henry Clay

Lincoln's political hero was Henry Clay and here his own head occupies the place where Clay's originally reposed.

No full length portrait of Lincoln seemed to be available at any time during his campaigns or administration, and these unusual lithographs are the results of artists' efforts to satisfy the public demand. The lithographer-artist in the above

Faked portraits of Abraham Lincoln.

full-length portrait available for distribution. To meet the public's demand, numerous artists adapted portraits of other people to become portraits of Lincoln. Perhaps the most famous Lincoln phony portrait is that which beheads the body of John C. Calhoun and replaces it with the head of Lincoln. This elegant,

Lincoln and Unknown

Some statesman of earlier days had his entire wearing apparel made over to harmonize with a later period and support the head of Lincoln.

Lincoln and John C. Calhoun

John C. Calhoun in this instance lost his head and the famous Brady portrait of Lincoln now adorns the shoulders.

cases worked from old steel engravings of other famous men, copied the picture on a lithograph stone and then drew in the head of Lincoln. The stone was then etched with acid and a lithograph made from it.

fake figure of Lincoln has often appeared on school classroom walls. Similar artistic surgery was performed on a portrait of Henry Clay. Sometimes, when an earlier statesman was transformed into Lincoln, that figure's whole costume was changed to make the attire suitably dignified for a President.

131

François Fournier and Jean de Sperati, Master Stamp Forgers

Today, over seventy years after his death, the name François Fournier still signifies a high point in stamp forgery. Between 1900 and his death in 1914, his stamp creations flooded the collecting world. He made 796 facsimile sets, which included 3,671 varieties of stamps, plus hundreds of fake cancellations, overprints, and surcharges.

To make a copy, or a facsimile, of a hard-to-find stamp is an accepted practice. However, unlike other facsimile-makers, Fournier refused to label his stamps as such in the prescribed way, by either marking them on the back or working the word "facsimile" into the design. In response to critics' accusations that he was trying to fool the public, Fournier replied that the marks would be aesthetically unacceptable or would be easy to remove. Fournier's copies were so good that unscrupulous dealers soon began to sell them as genuine first editions.

Fournier claimed his only purpose in creating copies of rare and expensive stamps was to give small collectors the chance to fill empty spaces in their albums. When Fournier continued to produce facsimiles, despite growing criticism from experts, the stamp collecting community grew hostile and filed lawsuits against him. At the beginning of World War I, his business was confiscated by the government, and he died in poverty. After the war, members of a stamp society gathered his remaining facsimiles and indelibly stamped them with the word "faux" or "facsimile" and put them into five hundred numbered albums. The society sold the albums for the equivalent of twenty-five dollars each. Today some of Fournier's albums are worth as much as one thousand dollars!

For half a century, another stamp forger, Jean de Sperati, an Italian by birth, but a resident of France, produced copies of old stamps so convincing that he fooled most experts. His success demanded he master the technical craft of making stamps. This includes finding the proper paper, ink, glue, and making the perforations (the notched edges of a stamp), as well as mastering the art of engraving images on the stamps. Jean de Sperati's facsimiles, like Fournier's, were so perfect, however, that they wreaked havoc upon the stamp collecting world as they were bought and sold by unsuspecting dealers and serious collectors. Finally, in 1954, in an unprecedented move, a British stamp collecting organization, the BPA, bought out Jean de Sperati. Thus ended the career of one of the master forgers of the century.

Detecting forgery in a piece of art requires instinct, training, and the availability of technical resources. At the same time, the resources available to the detective are also available to forgers, making it likely that current forgers are quietly at work somewhere, creating new fraudulent masterpieces. In auction showrooms today, art collectors often bid for authentic art in four, five, six and even seven figures, making the potential rewards of a successful forgery enormous.

CHAPTER EIGHT

SCIENTIFIC HOAXES

A Human Baby Created in a Laboratory Has Now Passed His
First Birthday

So reads the jacket flap of David Rorvik's controversial 1978 book *In His Image: The Cloning of a Man*. According to Rorvik, he had acted as an intermediary in a unique experiment to produce a baby that was the exact genetic twin of its parent—in other words, a clone.

In his book, Rorvik reports how an elderly millionaire, known only by the code name Max, contacted him and enlisted his assistance in finding a gynecologist willing to participate in this highly secret project. Rorvik located such a gynecologist, described only by his code name Darwin. Darwin was flown to an unidentified location in the tropics, where Max owned rubber plantations, nutmeg trees, and rice paddies. Under Darwin's guidance, Max had a hospital constructed and filled its rooms with women willing to act as surrogate mothers.

To accomplish the experiment, the cloned embryo was placed in the womb of one of these women. Rorvik describes the course of the pregnancy in meticulous detail, ending his book with the birth of the first cloned child in the world, in December, 1976, to a woman codenamed Sparrow.

As soon as Rorvik's book was published, people everywhere became entranced with the idea of cloning. If such a technique really worked, then everyone could produce identical copies of him or herself. The technique might even be used to "recreate" people who had died. The entire prospect was both horrifying and fascinating.

Numerous ethical questions surrounded the cloning of human beings. Was it possible that hospitals would be turned into human "copy machines," churning out multiple people to order? The spectre of a world full of clones prompted many scientists to promote the banning of all cloning experiments on humans.

One of the most frustrating aspects of Rorvik's book was his steadfast refusal to reveal the name or present location of any individual mentioned in the text. Rorvik claimed his reticence was due to his desire to "protect the child from harmful publicity."

Shortly after *In His Image* was published, an Oxford University geneticist, J. Derek Bromhall, filed a lawsuit against Rorvik. Bromhall charged that the book was a hoax and that the cloning technique described in the book was developed by Bromhall himself in his work on rabbits. Bromhall also accused Rorvik of using his name in the book without his permission.

Although Rorvik conceded that three of the minor characters in his book were invented, he maintained that the rest of the story was true. He still refused to produce either Max or the child, but did offer to supply blood samples from them both for testing. The court rejected the offer, as there was no guarantee that such samples would not be faked. In June, 1981, the judge of the U.S. District Court in Philadelphia ruled that the book was a "fraud and a hoax."

Through Rorvik's book, the word "clone" has become part of our common vocabulary and has provided the basis for countless cartoons and jokes. The boy clone hoax appealed to the public imagination because it was an idea that many people wished could be true.

For the moment, however, real human cloning remains the stuff of science fiction. Yet, in the same way that many amazing feats of modern technology were first explored in science fiction books, so too a day might come when, protected by safe and ethical guidelines, the main events of *In His Image* will be enacted in real life.

Fudging Facts in Modern Science

In the past, such great scientists as Claudius Ptolemy, Isaac Newton, and Gregor Mendel are said to have fudged some of their data. In the modern scientific world, experiments are carefully monitored, and researchers are under regular scrutiny from their peers. Yet, in the quest for truth, it occasionally happens that truth is bent or facts invented.

More recently, a prominent English psychologist who created influential theories about the development of human intelligence in the 1950s and 1960s, appears not only to have invented some of his data, but also to have created imaginary scientists as his collaborators. In 1974, it was revealed that a cancer researcher in the United States, had painted his mice to make it appear that his skin graft experiment had been successful. In 1982, another scientist was observed to falsify his report on a heart experiment by changing both the time and the results of the experiment.

Every year new cases of scientific fraud appear, and careers are jeopardized. Why? One reason is that the pressure to succeed in the competitive world of science is so intense that it is often easier and less time-consuming to falsify data than to pursue the scientific method. Also, it is sometimes difficult to collect sufficient data, and often it is tedious to repeat a long experiment in order to confirm previously established results.

In addition, scientific experiments rarely turn out perfectly. Often some results do not fit the pattern, and some scientists find it easier to ignore these results than to discover their cause. Bending the facts to fit a particularly attractive theory is tempting. However, a false theory can be dangerous when it provides the basis for further work.

Most scientists agree that the falsification of data is no more common now than it ever has been, but that the public is more aware of it because of increased media coverage. In the past, both the gaps in scientific knowledge and a less-educated public made it easier to perpetuate scientific hoaxes.

The Cardiff Giant

Today, in the Farmers' Museum in Cooperstown, New York, rests a larger-than-life reclining stone figure known as the Cardiff giant. This figure, whose rough-hewn features and oversize limbs were supposed to provide proof of the existence of giants in ancient times, played a central role in one of the most successful hoaxes of all time. Thousands came to see the figure, including many eminent scholars and clergymen. Even after the giant was declared a fake, the public continued to be fascinated by it, and for many years people thronged to view both the original Cardiff giant and its imitation exhibited by P. T. Barnum.

The "discovery" of the 2,999 pound giant occurred on Saturday, October 16, 1869, on a farm owned by a man named Stub Newell near the small town of Cardiff, New York. Newell hired some men to dig a well behind his barn. They had dug about five feet into the ground when their shovels uncovered what at first appeared to be a large rock. But as more of the rock

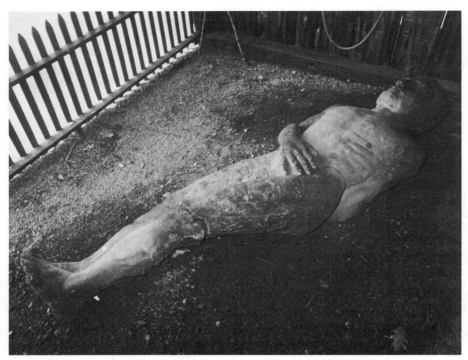

The Cardiff giant on display at the Farmer's Museum, Coopers-town, New York.

emerged, the realistic naked figure of a large stone man began to appear.

News of this amazing discovery spread almost instantly, and within hours a large crowd had gathered around the pit. People could hardly believe their eyes. Here was not a skeleton, but a complete figure of a very large, stockily built man, who apparently had been turned to stone. The surface of the stone was stained, suggesting that the figure had lain in the earth a long time. People in the area were accustomed to finding arrowheads and fossils of small animals such as fish and lizards, but no one had ever found any human remains, not to mention a giant stone human.

By Sunday, even more people came to see the giant, and by Monday, Stub Newell had erected a tent over the pit and was charging fifty-cents admission. Over the next two weeks, until the giant was moved on November 5, it attracted an average of three hundred to five hundred visitors a day. On one Sunday alone, twenty-six hundred tickets were sold!

Most people stood in awe of the figure. What was this giant? they wondered. How did it come to be buried on Stub Newell's farm? Although many people were willing and eager to believe that the giant was indeed a petrified man, the Cardiff giant was, in fact, a well-planned hoax, executed by a renowned scoundrel named George Hull.

George Hull first conceived of making a fake giant in 1866 when he was employed as a cigar manufacturer in Binghamton, New York. He had sent ten thousand cigars to his brother-in-law in Ackly, Iowa, to sell there. When his brother-in-law did not pay him, Hull traveled to Iowa to investigate. While staying with his sister and brother-in-law, Hull met a traveling preacher named Reverend Turk, with whom he got involved in lengthy discussions about whether or not there were giants in Biblical times. According to Turk, there must have been giants, for it was stated so in the Bible in the book of Genesis.

Hull returned to Iowa in 1868 to set up arrangements for the making of a giant. Not only did he want to make fools out of religionists such as Turk, but he figured he could make some money as well. On June 5, 1868, Hull and a partner, H. B. Martin, went to the gypsum quarries near Fort Dodge, Iowa. There they hired a man to cut out a block measuring twelve feet by four feet by twenty-two inches. Then they shipped the block to Chicago, where for three months, two sculptors, Henry Salle and Fred Mohrmann, carved it into the shape of a man. It is said that Hull himself was the model for the statue's features. Hull guarded his project carefully, covering the walls of the studio with carpets and quilts to deaden the sounds to passersby.

Hull realized the sculpture must look as real as possible if it were to pass as a petrified man. Thus, when he learned that hair does not petrify, he ordered the hair and beard on the sculpture to be chipped away. To make the skin look realistic, he fastened hundreds of darning needles to a block of wood and then pounded the surface of the stone to make it look as if the skin had pores.

After the sculpture was carved, it needed to be aged. Hull first rubbed the surface with a sponge filled with wet sand. Then he washed the sculpture with ink to darken the surface. When the ink stained too deeply, however, he was forced to lighten it with sulphuric acid. This, finally, created a suitable ancient effect.

At last the sculpture was ready to be buried, and Hull decided to use the farmland of a relative in Cardiff, New York. Better still, Hull knew his relative—Stub Newell—would go along with his plan. The giant was first shipped by rail to Broome County, New York, and from there loaded onto a wagon and taken by back roads to Cardiff. The figure was delivered to Stub Newell's farm in the dead of night, on November 9, 1868, and buried two weeks later. Then George Hull returned to his cigar-making business and waited a year for his plan to ripen. When the giant finally was discovered, the figure became a news sensation almost overnight.

As soon as the giant was unearthed, people split into various camps depending upon their beliefs. Some scientists, such as Professor O. C. Marsh of Yale University and Andrew D. White of Cornell University, declared the giant a fraud. Others believed firmly in the theory of petrifaction, that is, that a body could turn to stone. Still others maintained the giant was an ancient statue. As long as the controversy raged, people remained interested in the giant.

For the small village of Cardiff, with its population of two hundred, the giant provided an economic boom not seen before or since. In 1869, Cardiff possessed a tannery, two blacksmiths, a wagon shop, two hotels, and a church. As tourists arrived to view the giant, local residents took advantage of the opportunity to earn more money. One newspaper estimated that the hotel did more business in four days than it normally did in four months. Taxi services to local train stops abounded. Many people sold gingerbread and apple cider in front of their homes, and two people, including Newell, opened informal restaurants.

After exhibiting the giant for a week or so, Hull realized that his joke would soon be revealed, and he contrived to sell three quarters of his share in the giant to a group of local businessmen for thirty thousand dollars. In just a few weeks in Cardiff, the giant made twelve thousand dollars for its investors. The businessmen then decided to move the giant from Newell's farm to Syracuse, New York. There, even more people came to view the petrified man. The local papers promoted the story with great enthusiasm, and their circulation increased enormously as a result.

Although local papers tended to discount any stories of the giant being a fraud, newspapers from other towns not lucky enough to have a giant of their own, were eager to uncover the real story. By December, 1869, their headlines reported that the Cardiff giant was a hoax. Paleontologists showed that the gypsum composing the giant was not a local stone. Moreover, if the figure had lain in the earth as long as presumed, the Cardiff giant would have been considerably more corroded. George Hull and Newell admitted their part in the scheme, and the two sculptors, Mohrmann and Salle, confessed to their part in the giant's creation.

Despite the exposure of the fraud, the Cardiff giant's reputation spread, and people still wanted to see it. Showman P. T. Barnum, unable to buy the real giant from its owners, had a new one carved so that for a time, there were two Cardiff giants being exhibited for the public's enjoyment. Other hoaxers were inspired by the Cardiff giant's success, and several other supposed petrified bodies revealed themselves. One, the Forest City Man from South Dakota, was exhibited at the Chicago World's Fair in 1893. Another, called The Colorado Man, created for P. T. Barnum, enjoyed a modest success until debunked by Yale's Professor Marsh. Today, more than one hundred years after the fake figure was unearthed, visitors still go to Cooperstown, New York, to see the original Cardiff giant—the object of one of the greatest hoaxes in history.

The Piltdown Man

The discovery of a few old bones and pieces of chipped flint in a gravel pit in Sussex, England, in 1912, may not seem to be a remarkable find. Yet these objects marked the beginning of a hoax that altered scientific thinking for nearly half a century. The bones, which included a human skull and an apelike jaw with human teeth, seemed to provide startling new evidence about human evolution. At a time when Charles Darwin's theories of evolution were just beginning to take hold, the discovery of the "missing link" between ape and human development was exactly the answer for which scientists were looking.

Up to that time, the oldest known human skeleton was that of the Neanderthal man, which had no apelike features. The new skeleton, named *Eoanthropus dawsoni* after its discoverer, Charles Dawson, was proclaimed to be much older and clearly had features of both ape and man.

Charles Dawson was a local Sussex solicitor whose hobby was paleontology. Throughout England fossils had been found in gravel pits and road cuttings. Dawson, like many others, made a hobby of collecting them. When he heard from some workmen repairing a road near Piltdown Common that they had uncovered a human bone, Dawson went to look for more. What he

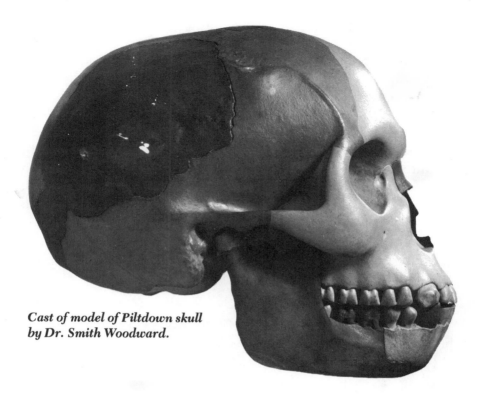

*Cast of model of Piltdown skull
by Dr. Smith Woodward.*

found was a thick human skull and an apelike jawbone. Both appeared to be about five hundred thousand years old.

He took his discoveries to the British Museum, where he showed them to Dr. Arthur Smith Woodward, head of the geology department. Woodward immediately recognized the importance of Dawson's discoveries and returned with him to the Piltdown site, accompanied by a third man, Teilhard de Chardin. Chardin was a young French Jesuit priest with an avid interest in paleontology. The men continued to dig. They found more bones, including those of animals such as elephants and hippopotami, and there were more flint tools. When Woodward published the results of their research in December 1912, he concluded with this sentence: "Dr. Smith Woodward accordingly inclines to the theory that the Neanderthal race was a degenerate offshoot of early Man, while surviving modern Man may have arisen directly from a primitive source of which the Piltdown skull provides the first discovered evidence."

Clearly this was a remarkable discovery. Yet, the famous skull, which became known as the Piltdown man, presented a puzzle to anthropologists, for it was a piece that simply did not fit into the other known facts about human evolution. Most people believed that the jaw and teeth began to evolve into their human form quite early in history, and that the enlarged

A discussion of the Piltdown skull by Mr. T.O. Barlow, Prof. Elliot Smith, Prof. A.S. Underwood, Prof. A. Kieth, Mr. Charles Dawson, Dr. Smith Woodward, Mr. W.P. Pycroft and Sir E. Ray Lancaster.

skull evolved later. However, the Piltdown skull suggested the opposite order of events. Some scientists developed elaborate new theories to make the Piltdown skull fit into the scheme of evolution. Others, such as those at the Museum of Natural History in New York, were skeptical from the beginning. Even though the skeptics disputed the interpretation of the evidence, no one at that time suspected that the evidence itself was a hoax.

Nearly forty years later, Dr. Kenneth Oakley, a British geologist, discovered that bones buried in the earth absorb the chemical fluorine from ground water. The longer the bones remain buried, the more fluorine they absorb. When, in 1949, Dr. Oakley used his knowledge to test the age of the Piltdown skull, he found it was much newer than the half a million years old that had previously been claimed.

When Dr. Oakley presented his findings to a group of paleontologists at a London conference in 1953, they decided to subject the skull to further examination. Using modern techniques, such as X-ray spectrography, geiger counter readings, and an improved chemical-dating test, they proved conclusively that the "ancient" jaw had come from a modern orangutan that had been artificially stained to create its old appearance. Telltale scratches on the molars showed those teeth had been filed to make them appear to be human teeth. Also, the forger had cleverly broken the hinge of the jaw so it would not be obvious that the jaw did not fit with the skull.

Who was this clever forger, and what was his motivation? Because the forgery had been so carefully prepared, the evidence pointed to someone with expert knowledge, and many believe that Piltdown man was created by one of those involved in its discovery. Dr. J. S. Weiner, in his book *The Piltdown Forgeries*, suggests that the culprit was Charles Dawson. Dawson was known to have had a laboratory in which he stained fossils in chemical solutions and once traded a bogus fossil with a friend. Dawson is a logical suspect, for he lived in the area and could easily have planted the fake fossils in the dig. He also had a large fossil collection that could have included the animal fossils such as those which accompanied the Piltdown skull.

As it turned out, many of the fossils found at the Piltdown site were not known to be native to that area. After the hoax was revealed, a careful examination showed that a fossil rhino tooth, supposedly found there, was from East Anglia; an elephant tooth was from Tunisia; and the orangutan jaw was from Borneo. Obviously, someone had planted them at the site. The amazing fact was that no one seriously questioned this strange collection of objects earlier.

Another possible suspect, suggested by anthropologist Louis Leakey, and more recently by Stephen Jay Gould of Harvard University, is Teilhard de Chardin, the Jesuit priest and philosopher. According to letters made public since his death in 1955, he may have known more about the Piltdown skull than he admitted during his lifetime. Even so, the evidence against Chardin is insubstantial especially since he met Dawson only after the first find of the Piltdown man hoax was made.

Perhaps the most unlikely, but certainly the most intriguing candidate for the Piltdown hoaxer is Sir Arthur Conan Doyle, creator of the Sherlock Holmes mystery stories. This theory has recently been suggested by researcher John Winslow. Not only did Doyle, who was trained as a medical doctor, have the knowledge necessary to perpetrate the hoax, but he was known to have been to the Piltdown site during the digging. Winslow suggests that Doyle may have wanted to play a joke on the scientific community, against which he felt a deep grudge.

As all the people who were involved in the Piltdown discoveries are now dead, all the questions about the deception most likely will never be answered. Yet, the Piltdown man remains one of the most fascinating and longest-running hoaxes of the twentieth century.

Sir Francis Drake's Brass Plaque

In 1936, when a small brass plaque discovered by a picnicker near San Francisco, California, was presented to the California Historical Society, it seemed to be the long lost evidence of the landing in northern California of world navigator, Sir Francis Drake, nearly four hundred years earlier.

When Drake set sail from England on December 13, 1577, he began what would become the first trip around the world by an Englishman. In the course of that journey, he sailed around

Originally attributed to English navigator, Sir Francis Drake, this plate of brass, which was found in California in 1936, was later declared a forgery.

the southern tip of South America and then up the west coast of both Americas, landing in 1579 somewhere along the California coast. According to an account written by the ship's chaplain, Francis Fletcher, Drake named his landing spot in North America New Albion. Apparently, he left a brass plaque at the site as his claim to the land. Although no proof exists of the exact landing spot, many believe that Drake anchored in a large sheltered bay about twenty-five miles north of San Francisco, now called Drake's Bay.

Then one day in 1936, a twenty-five-year-old bank clerk named Beryle Shinn was having a picnic in Greenbrae, a small town in Marin County, just north of San Francisco. When he idly turned over a rock, he discovered a rectangular piece of metal, about five-by-seven-inches big. At the time, Shinn did not look at the piece carefully, but rather stuck it over a hole in the floor of his car. Several months later, when he repaired his car, Shinn removed the metal plate and washed it. Much to his surprise, he discovered the plate was covered with a strange, unreadable inscription. On the advice of a friend, Shinn turned over the plaque to Dr. Herbert Eugene Bolton, an expert in California history and director of the Bancroft Library in Berkeley.

Bolton deciphered the inscription which read:

> Be it knowne unto all men by these presents June 17, 1579
> By the grace of God and in the name of Herr Majesty Queen
> Elizabeth of England and her successors forever I take possession
> of this kingdome whose king and people freely resigne their right
> and title in the whole land unto Herr Maiesties keeping now
> named by me and to bee knowne unto all men as Nova Albion
> Francis Drake

At last it appeared that the brass plaque described by Fletcher had been found. When the news of the plaque was publicized, a chauffeur came forward and claimed to have originally found it at Drake's Bay, and then discarded the plaque near Greenbrae. To prove the plaque's authenticity, the piece was sent to metal experts at Columbia University in New York. All verified that the metal was quite old, and thus the plaque was installed at the Bancroft Library as a genuine California relic.

Nevertheless, some people still had nagging doubts about the genuineness of the plaque. Some British historians felt that the language of the inscription was too modern in some places, and the spellings were odd. Others, such as noted naval historian Samuel Eliot Morison of Harvard University, also pronounced the plate a fake.

In preparation for the four hundredth anniversary of Drake's landing, a new investigation of the plate was ordered. When the results were published in July 1977, the headlines read, "Drake's Plate Is a Fake." New methods of testing had shown that the brass used for the plate had been rolled, a technique not known in Drake's time. The edges had also been cut, not chiseled, as they would have been in the sixteenth century.

The mystery of why such a hoax was perpetrated has not been solved. It has been suggested that some of Dr. Bolton's students created the plaque but, when they realized how devastated Dr. Bolton would be to discover the plaque was a fake, decided to keep quiet. Dr. Bolton died in 1953, believing the plaque to be genuine. Today the plaque remains on display at the Bancroft Library, along with the story of the detective work that revealed it as a fake. Sir Frances Drake's Plaque continues to draw many visitors.

Hoaxes or Not?

Thousands of forged antiques turn up every year. Any archeologist would be able to detect these frauds in a minute. At the same time, there have been some finds that were declared false at first, which later turned out to be genuine.

The Kensington Runestone is a slab of sandstone carved with old Norse letters. A Minnesota farmer, Olof Ohman, found the stone in 1898, which seemed to provide proof that Viking explorers came to America before Columbus. After a professor at Northwestern University declared the stone to be a fake however, the Ohmans turned the stone into a doorstep to their farm granary. Today, more recent discoveries of Viking tools and weapons in North America suggest that the stone is genuine. In 1947, the Kensington Runestone was sent to the Smithsonian Institution in Washington, D.C. As with many unusual discoveries, there are those who still believe that the Kensington Runestone is a hoax. If so, it is a deception which was cleverly devised.

Twenty-six years after the Kensington Runestone discovery, a young farm boy was plowing a field near the tiny village of Glozel, France, when his oxen suddenly fell into a large hole. When the boy went to investigate, he discovered that the bottom of the hole was a large oval area paved with large flat stones, seemingly the remnant of some ancient society. Although the stones turned out to be part of a medieval glass furnace, further digging around the site revealed a large and confusing array of Stone Age artifacts, including stone axes, carved bones, and pebbles. Most intriguing of all, there were several clay tablets carved with indecipherable "letters."

Like the Kensington Runestone, the Glozel discoveries became the center of great controversy. Some scientists instantly pronounced them a hoax. After all, they said, no artifacts of a similar nature had ever been found in that region before. If the objects were genuine, then the whole course of man's early history in Europe would have to be rewritten. Other scientists were equally convinced that the artifacts were genuine. One of these was Dr. Salomon Reinach, director of the Museum of National Antiquities in France. He wrote, "Glozel is a transition period between the 'reindeer age' and the age of metal. Men of that period had, at least in the foothills of Auvergne, a developed form of writing, an alphabet which should be dated well before the Phoenician script."

Dr. Reinach pointed out that some of the objects, such as an idol in the shape of a violin, were similar to those of Neolithic cultures in the Aegean. And if the alphabet tablets were genuine, many theories of the origin of the alphabet would have to be revised.

To settle the argument over the authenticity of the Glozel finds, the International Anthropological Congress appointed a commission to investigate the case. In November, 1927, the Congress sent seven of their members to spend three days on the site. After doing some digging of their own and examining the objects already found at Glozel, the commission declared that everything except a few stone axes were forgeries.

Despite the lack of confidence by the rest of the scientific world, some scientists, including Dr. Reinach, continued to dig at Glozel. He uncovered more objects, including a new alphabet tablet. These investigations continued until 1942, when France was occupied by Nazi Germany.

After that time, most people seemed to forget about Glozel. Then in 1974, a group of scientists decided to use a new technique called thermoluminescence to try to date some of the objects from the Glozel site.

Thermoluminescence is useful for dating objects made of clay. In its raw state, clay stores huge amounts of energy, accumulated over long periods of time, from radiation in the environment. When the clay is made into a pot and fired, that is, heated to a high temperature in a kiln, this energy is "erased." After firing, the clay begins to reaccumulate energy again. In the laboratory, small bits of ancient clay objects can be heated until they glow. By measuring the strength of the glow, the age of the piece can then be calculated.

When the Glozel artifacts were subjected to these tests, they were shown to have been made between 700 B.C. and 100 A.D. Thus, the thermoluminescence tests provided evidence that they were not forgeries after all. Nevertheless, how they came to be buried in Glozel, and what they signify remains unsolved.

A Shroud of Mystery

Since early Christian times the faithful have made pilgrimages to venerate relics of holy figures. Perhaps the most precious of these relics is a three-and-a-half-by-fourteen-foot strip of linen, which is supposedly the burial cloth of Jesus Christ. The cloth, known as the Shroud of Turin, is kept in the Royal Chapel of the Cathedral of St. John, in the northern Italian city of Turin. The relic is locked in a double chest that can only be opened by using three different keys.

The most unusual and mysterious feature of the shroud is that it bears a life-size image of a bearded man whose hands and body bear witness to a death by crucifixion. The identity of the figure and how the image came to be part of the cloth, are mysteries that have perplexed scientists and historians for at least two hundred years. Although some evidence points to the possibility that the cloth may be genuine, some believe the shroud is a forgery, probably by a fourteenth-century artist. The lack of smeared bloodstains, as well as the fact that the bloodstains indicate that the figure was vertical when wrapped, rather than horizontal, as one would expect a corpse to be, suggest forgery. So does the forked beard, a common style in the Middle Ages, but not in the time of Jesus.

No one has yet been able to prove how such an image could be impressed onto cloth. Various attempts to create a similar image, such as wrapping cloth around a heated statue, have failed. Believers suggest the image could only have been the result of a miraculous flash of radiation occurring at the moment of resurrection.

In 1978, the Vatican made the shroud available to a team of scientists for five days of examination. It was hoped they would be able to provide some new answers to the old mystery. More than twenty-five scientists, all part of the Shroud of Turin Research Project, gathered in a specially prepared room in the royal palace adjacent to the Turin Cathedral. There they watched as the shroud was taken out of its protective casket for just the ninth time in the last two hundred years. Then they began to subject the shroud to the closest scrutiny technology could offer.

First the shroud was photographed in meticulous detail, using techniques that varied from photomicrography, ultraviolet and infrared light, and low energy x-ray radiation, to ordinary light photography. Then the team collected bits of fibers, dust particles, and pollen which had collected on the surface of the cloth. These were used in further physical and chemical tests.

When examined, some of the pollen was discovered to have come from plants found only in the area around the Dead Sea, indicating that the cloth may have been in the Middle East at some point in its history. Before the fourteenth century, when the shroud first surfaced in the family of a French knight known as Geoffrey de Charny, the background of the shroud is murky. However, some people believe that before its discovery in France, the shroud was taken from its tomb in Palestine to Turkey, then to Constantinople, and from there to France. No one will ever know for certain unless some previously unknown manuscript emerges to tell the shroud's true story.

At first people thought that a clever artist had simply painted the image onto the cloth. Yet a careful examination with microscopes revealed no telltale brushmarks. Others thought the image was burned into the fibers. Yet, when the shroud was examined with ultraviolet light, the only areas that revealed burning were the sections of the cloth that had been scorched in a fire in 1532.

One intriguing feature of the image is that it becomes much clearer when looked at in a photographic negative. This discovery, made around the turn of this century by an amateur Italian photographer, suggests that the cloth itself is like a piece of photographic film. To test this theory, one scientist, Samuel Pellicori, rubbed onto his hands a mixture of body oils, sweat, and ancient burial ointments such as olive oil and myrrh. Then he pressed his hands onto a piece of linen. When he baked the linen to simulate aging, the linen discolored in the places where he had pressed his hands. Although this experiment suggested one way the cloth may have been marked, it did not explain the extraordinary clarity of the facial features.

The preliminary report of the research team's findings was finished in 1981 and presented to the archbishop and to the owner of the shroud, the exiled King Umberto II of Italy. As of 1986, the final report has not been made, and scientists are still waiting for permission from the pope to use carbon-dating techniques to determine the age of the cloth more precisely. As one member of the research team pointed out however, "People who have faith don't need a relic or an icon or an image. People who don't have faith aren't going to buy it even if we could prove that it was Christ, which no one will ever be able to do. It's still a matter of faith."

CHAPTER NINE

HOAXES JUST FOR FUN

On a bitter cold morning in December, 1983, while most of the citizens in Milwaukee, Wisconsin, stayed indoors not daring to venture forth into the below-freezing temperature, two dozen people ransacked their houses for baseball mitts and hurried to County Stadium. They waited for hours in the freezing cold, braving frost bite, pneumonia, and a wind-chill factor of minus two degrees. No sports event was scheduled for County Stadium that day, but there *was* another event worth the chilling wait.

That morning, two disc jockeys, Gene Mueller and Bob Reitman, had announced over Station WKTI, Milwaukee, that anyone willing to participate in an American Express commercial, to be filmed by helicopter at County Stadium, would be given a free gift. All they had to do was wave their American

Helicopter arriving with Cabbage Patch Kids® dolls.

(Cabbage Patch Kids® is a Registered Trademark of Original Appalachian Artwork, Inc.)

Delivering the Cabbage Patch Kids® dolls.

Receiving the Cabbage Patch Kids® dolls.

Recipients of Cabbage Patch Kids® dolls in 1984, with Gene Mueller (left) and Bob Reitman (right).

Express cards at the helicopter when it flew overhead. "And be sure," the disc jockeys added, "to bring a catcher's mitt, because a B59 bomber will drop two thousand of these prized, free gifts into the middle of the stadium."

Later, when neither the helicopter nor the B59 showed up, the disc jockeys admitted that both the commercial and the free gifts were a hoax. Even so, many people refused to leave, afraid that the revealing of the hoax was another trick, and they'd miss out on their free gift.

What was this prize that kept twenty-four people voluntarily freezing for hours? It was America's hottest new fad item, the most sought after toy since the hula hoop craze of the 1960s— the Cabbage Patch Kids doll.

The Cabbage Patch Drop, as the hoax came to be called, eventually had a happy footnote. Mueller and Reitman said they never expected anyone to fall for their gag and were shocked when people actually showed up. As most stores had already sold out of the dolls, the disc jockeys admitted feeling a bit guilty for squelching people's hopes of finding one in time for Christmas.

To make amends, the next year the disc jockeys made the same announcement. This time, however, the joke was on the nonbelievers. For, although the dolls were delivered by helicopter, not a B59 bomber, and the chopper landed before dropping off its priceless cargo, the recipients did receive their free Cabbage Patch Kids dolls. Mueller and Reitman gave their hoax a happy ending.

Practical Jokes

Hoaxes played just for the fun of it are sometimes called practical jokes. Whereas a comedian relies upon the effect of his or her punch line to get laughs, a practical joker relies upon creating a funny situation. Sometimes a joker sees a person in an everyday activity, such as going to the supermarket, and suddenly he or she thinks of a way of turning this ordinary event into a prank.

Before the *Dreadnought* Affair, Horace deVere Cole played several spur-of-the-moment practical jokes. Once, on his way home from buying a ball of twine, he saw such an elegantly dressed man that he could not resist spoofing him. Cole pretended to be a surveyor in the process of realigning the curb. He told the man that his assistant had disappeared and asked if the gentleman could help him by holding the end of the twine. The man agreed and Cole handed him one end of the string and then started backing away, unwinding the ball as he went. When the string was completely unraveled, Cole saw another man dressed as elegantly as the first. Cole asked him if he would help with an engineering project, and the gentleman agreed. Cole gave him the other end of the twine and told him to hold it and not move. Then Cole disappeared around a corner and went home.

Another on-the-spot ruse occurred in London one morning, when two British comedians, known as Flanagan and Allen, were on their way to play golf. They saw some workmen putting up a mailbox on a corner. The comedians rushed to the men.

"You're putting the box on the wrong corner," Allen exclaimed, panting.

One of the workmen looked at his blueprint. "But the northeast corner is marked on the plans," he insisted.

"It shouldn't be," argued Flanagan. "We're from the city planning office, and the box goes on the northwest corner."

The comedian/hoaxers pretended to examine the plans, then told the workmen that the person who signed the plans had made another of his boo-boos. Allen marked out "northeast" and penciled in northwest. Then the comedians got back in their car and drove to the golf course. The mailbox still stands on the northwest corner today.

Hugh Troy, an American artist and illustrator, was a prolific practical joker and acquired such a great reputation perpetrating pranks that the American comedian Harpo Marx called him "the most eminent practitioner of the art." Because Hugh frequently found his reputation a hindrance, he often played practical jokes anonymously. He claimed he put together one of his favorite hoaxes in the following way.

In 1935, when the Museum of Modern Art in New York City held an exhibit of Van Gogh paintings, Hugh became annoyed at the unusually large crowd that prevented him from getting a good view of the exhibit. Hugh suspected most of the people were there because of the recently published bizarre details of Van Gogh's life, in particular, the artist's cutting off his ear. To test his theory, Hugh carved a fake ear out of dried beef, mounted it in a velvet box, and labeled the ear as Van Gogh's. Surreptitiously he smuggled the box into the museum and placed it on a table in the room where the Van Gogh paintings were hung. Soon the crowd swarmed around the ear exhibit, ignoring Van Gogh's paintings, which Hugh now enjoyed in semiprivacy and peace.

On another occasion, Hugh was among a group of artists and entertainers who were invited to a charity carnival and auction on the estate of an extremely arrogant woman. The guests at the carnival were the cream of high society. Each artist was taken to meet the woman, who promptly said, "I am giving two minutes to each of you people. You are to paint a picture for the auction. Now your two minutes are up. Kindly leave."

Hugh felt so outraged at the woman's behavior, that instead of painting a picture to be auctioned he painted several signs, which he nailed around the estate's entrance. The signs said:

> Picnic Parties Welcome
> Basket Parties Invited
> Free Merry-go-round for the Children
> Lemonade for All

Hugh then hitched a ride back to New York, leaving the arrogant hostess and her exclusive guests to deal with the "party crashers."

An extraordinary hoax occurred in New York City during the summer of 1824 when a retired carpenter named Lozier fooled practically all of Manhattan. Lozier managed to get an appointment with the mayor to discuss the "tragic condition" of Manhattan Island, which he said was sinking into the sea due to the weight of the tall buildings at the Battery end. The evidence could be seen, Lozier added, by the fact that the streets ran downhill all the way from City Hall to the Battery. The entire island could break off and fall into the sea at any moment.

Lozier suggested workers saw off the Manhattan Island at the Battery end, row it into the bay, turn it around, row it back, then re-attach Manhattan to the mainland by its opposite, stronger end. The mayor believed in the opinion of the respected carpenter and gave Lozier full control over the project.

Excitement rose with the same speed that unemployment dropped. Lozier hired three hundred men to saw and row, and contracted a small army of carpenters to build barracks to house the workers. He ordered herds of live cattle, chickens, and hogs to feed the crew, which the butchers sent to the docks alive, to be slaughtered as needed.

On the appointed day, practically everyone in Manhattan showed up to watch. Everyone, that is, except Lozier. After hours of waiting, while the cattle mooed, hogs squealed, and chickens cackled, the angry crowd left. Eventually someone discovered a note from Lozier saying he had to leave town unexpectedly for health reasons. A posse formed to find the hoaxer, but Lozier had already skipped out.

Yet another hoax has been played so many times that it has become practically a tradition at summer camps. This is the snipe hunt, first invented in rural America where it was played on visitors from the city.

To begin the prank, old-time campers and counselors tell new campers they're going on a snipe hunt at night. They instruct the newcomers to bring a flashlight and a paper bag. That night they sneak into the woods, where the counselors explain the snipe lives under bushes and is very shy. The bird won't come out unless the camper keeps yelling, "Here Snipe!" while beating on the bushes with the flashlight. The camper must hold the bag ready to catch the snipe when it runs out. Then the counselors say they are going to look for some snipe in another part of the woods, and everyone should meet back at the cabins as soon as they have caught a snipe. Actually, the counselors and old-time campers go back to the cabins leaving the new campers "holding the bag."

In the tradition of college student practical jokes, perhaps none are so ambitious as the students of California Institute of Technology's annual New Year's Day Rose Bowl pranks. The students take delight in sabotaging some portion of the festivities so that the public's attention is momentarily diverted from the football game to Cal Tech. When successful, their ingenuity is seen by billions on national television.

Their first large success was in 1961 when the Washington Huskies were playing the Minnesota Gophers. It began when a Cal Tech student, posing as a high school reporter, interviewed the card section of the Washington spirit squad and learned the details of the card routines. The night before the game, when everyone in the spirit squad was out, the Cal Tech people sneaked into the Washington rooms and changed the master sheets for two of the card stunts.

The next day the Washington students went to the Rose Bowl, and at half time, enthusiastically thrust their cards over their heads. However, instead of producing a picture of a Huskie as planned, a Cal Tech beaver emerged. No one could figure out what was wrong. Quickly, the leader instructed the students to go on to the next formation. They thrust up their cards again. This time it was supposed to read "Washington" but instead, the huge letters read "Cal Tech." The fans cheered when they realized the joke. The Beavers had outfoxed the Huskies.

In 1984 the Cal Tech students took on Rose Bowl security by

tapping into the scoreboard via two microprocessor units. One of the units was planted at the stadium, and the other was stationed about two miles away. As the game proceeded, the UCLA football players hammered away at the Illinois team. Then, with five minutes and ten seconds remaining, and the score at UCLA–38, Illinois–9, Cal Tech struck. They switched on the microprocessors and changed the scoreboard to read Cal Tech–38, MIT–9. In the lower right hand corner they detailed two beavers. Rose Bowl authorities did not have time to undo the trick before the end of the game, and in exasperation, simply turned the whole scoreboard off. Again, Cal Tech got national television coverage.

Although not all Cal Tech pranks have been so wildly successful as these, each year Rose Bowl authorities are wary of what Cal Tech ingenuity might think of next.

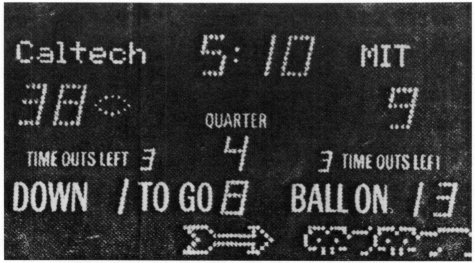

A group of students from Cal Tech succeeded in changing the scoreboard during the 1984 UCLA-Illinois Rose Bowl game. The arrow at the bottom of the board is pointing to two beavers, the Cal Tech mascot.

Telephone Pranks

It is said that no one person has done more for the practical joke than Alexander Graham Bell. Almost everyone who has played a prank for fun has used the telephone at least once as the means to fool another.

Perhaps one of the oldest telephone pranks is calling a number at random and asking, "Is your refrigerator running?" When the person answers "yes," the joker replies, "Well, you'd better run and catch it!"

Other phone pranks involve a responding action from the person being fooled. During the 1920s, when Mr. Bell's invention was still a novelty to most people, a prankster phoned a few of his friends and, disguising his voice, said he was the telephone engineer. On Saturday the telephone company planned to clean the lines using a machine that blew down through the lines and spewed out the dirt. He was calling to warn the person to put the receiver into a paper bag on Saturday, so dirt blown out of the phone lines wouldn't scatter all over the house.

On Saturday the jokester dropped by each of his friends' houses. He found them staying in the same room with their telephone. While keeping their distance from the phone, they watched the instrument intently, listening for a sound which would indicate the cleaning process had begun. They refused to answer their phone when it rang, afraid they would get a faceful of soot. Supposedly the only person who answered his telephone that afternoon was a Dr. Gerrity, who, without even saying hello, roared, "Don't call this number don't you know the phone company's blowing out the lines this afternoon!"

Phony Invitations for Phony Occasions

In 1845, invitations to the "Annual Ceremony of Washing the White Lions in London Tower" were sent to many prominent Londoners. Guards at the Tower accused the Londoners of lunacy when they arrived waving their invitations and demanding to be taken to the washing site. Many red faces returned home when the guards explained there was no such lion-washing ceremony.

Sending out bogus invitations to parades, banquets, unveil-ings, and other phony functions has always been a popular practical joke. Sometimes a prankster's sole motive in playing this type of hoax is to expose the foolishness of others when the prank is revealed.

For example, a reporter on the Paris newspaper *L'Eclair* saw a cabinet minister dedicate statues to a musician and a philoso-pher on the same day. The politician used practically the same speech for each ceremony. The reporter thought how foolish the minister was to believe the men being honored would not know the difference. To prove his point, the reporter invented an historical hero named Hegesippe Simon and sent printed invitations to the French National Assembly, inviting its mem-bers to speak at the unveiling of a monument dedicated to Simon's memory. The reporter called the hero the "precursor of modern democracy, and martyr to the tyranny of the *ancien regime*." Twenty-four assemblymen accepted, many sending letters expressing their gratitude for the opportunity to speak about this "educator of democracy." When *L'Eclair* exposed the hoax and printed the letters, the assemblymen received some "dedicated tyranny" of their own.

College campuses seem to sprout practical jokes like weeds in a garden. The editors of Cornell University's student newspa-per, *The Sun*, once invented a personality named Hugo N. Frye and claimed he founded the Republican Party in New York State. Then the students sent phony invitations for a banquet honoring Frye's one hundred and fiftieth birthday to congress-men, senators, and members of the president's cabinet. The invitation included Frye's supposed slogans, which were "Pro-tection for our prosperity" and "Freedom in the land of the free."

Most recipients declined but nevertheless wrote letters expressing appreciation that this great man was being honored. One person wrote: "It is a pleasure to testify to the career of that sturdy patriot who first painted the ideals of our party in this region of the country."

When the Cornell *Sun* revealed the hoax, they told readers to pronounce the name Hugo N. Frye out loud.

Misleading Evidence

Another type of hoax just for fun is the manufacture of misleading evidence to fool others. While in college, the trickster Hugh Troy conceived the idea for a prank when he saw a friend's wastebasket made in the shape of a rhinoceros foot. Borrowing the wastebasket, Hugh made rhinoceros footprints around the snow-covered campus, stopping at the frozen lake, where there was a hole in the ice, so it seemed the animal had fallen into the lake and drowned.

The local paper fell for the hoax and printed the story. Authorities called every zookeeper in the Northeastern United States to ask if a rhinoceros was missing from their zoos. Despite zookeepers' assurances to the contrary, citizens living nearby eagerly waited for the ice to melt so the lake could be dredged for the rhinoceros' frozen body.

Most practical jokes are remembered because of their success in fooling others. Yet sometimes the best-laid hoaxes are recalled for their failure to fool. For example, once some college students attached dragonfly wings, a cricket's head, and a tadpole's tail to the body of a spider. Then they asked their biology professor to identify the mysterious insect. The professor examined the specimen and said, "This is very interesting. Was it humming when you saw it?"

A resounding yes came from the students.

"In that case," the professor replied, "I think it must be a *hum* bug."

Hoaxers For Hire

One professional hoaxer was William Stanley Sims, who specialized in spoofing people at conventions. Once he gave a long, involved speech to the Gourmet Society on how to make an omelette flambé. Sims then proceeded to cook his creation, providing a bang of a finish when the omelette exploded on stage. Another time, he lectured the National Convention of Undertakers, where he pretended to be an authority on Egyptian embalming practices. Sims embalmed a corpse as a demonstration, at the end of which the corpse sat up and waved to the audience.

At a meeting of the American College of Surgeons, Sims was hired to be Dr. Eric Von Austerlitz, a distinguished Viennese surgeon. Sims spoke in rapid, medical jargon to describe a complicated operation he had supposedly performed, concluding with: "In short, I removed the patient's entire alimentary canal, turned it upside down, and stitched it back into position." The audience gasped, and Sims thought his imposture had failed until one of the doctors asked in total seriousness: "What was the patient's complaint?" With a straight face, Sims answered, "Hiccups."

In 1952, Hugh Troy got into the business of hoaxers for hire. When the American University in Washington, D.C., began a course in ghostwriting, Troy placed this ad in the *Washington Post*:

> Too Busy to Paint? Call on the Ghost Artists. 1426 33rd Street, N.W. We paint it, you sign it. Primitive (Grandma Moses type), impressionist, modern, cubist, abstract, sculpture. Why not give an exhibition?

When questioned by reporters, Troy boasted that his business had opened this branch in Washington because so many government employees demanded his services. However, for once the joke was on Hugh Troy when bundles of letters arrived from people who wanted Troy to paint a masterpiece for them to sign as their own. In addition, real art forgers started advertising in the newspaper for clients. Hugh quickly turned in his oil paints.

When Hugh Troy was in Officers' Training School during World War II, he felt that writing detailed reports about insignificant camp operations involved enormous amounts of unnecessary paperwork. He decided to bring the "everything in triplicate" to a status *ad absurdum*. Hugh Troy invented his own report, wrote up a form, and mimeographed copies. Then he filled in one of his forms each day and sent it to the Pentagon. Hugh called his report Fly-paper Effectiveness. Among the many questions he included in his fake form, were the number of flies caught by each strip of fly-paper in the mess hall, the positioning of each strip, and the weather conditions on each day.

Shortly thereafter Hugh left the camp with his unit and never learned when the camp stopped sending in the Fly-paper Reports, if ever.

P. T. Barnum

Phineas Taylor Barnum is probably best known for his Greatest Show on Earth—the circus he opened in 1850, in Brooklyn, New York. Yet Barnum was also a master showman in perpetrating hoaxes just for fun. He was an expert at judging what phony creatures would fool the public and thus attract the most paying customers.

Of his fabulous fakes, Joice Heth, was one of the best known attractions. Barnum claimed the woman was 161 years old and had been the nurse of George Washington. Although Joice looked ancient, with wrinkled, sagging skin, when she eventually died an autopsy proved she was no older than eighty.

The Light of Asia was an elephant Barnum painted white to fool the public into believing the animal was a valuable white elephant from Siam. The paint washed off every time it rained however, and Barnum had to give up on that deception.

The Feejee Mermaid, which Barnum claimed was from Calcutta, was a phony sea urchin constructed by grafting together a monkey's torso to a fish's tail. Barnum displayed advertisements showing the "mermaid" in Feejee, swimming in her native habitat before being captured.

So many of Barnum's exhibits were fakes, that many people assumed all his exhibits were hoaxes. However, a few of his discoveries were genuine. Barnum's popular dwarfs, Tom Thumb, three-feet, four-inches tall, and Jenny Lind, the tiny opera singer, were everything Barnum advertised them to be. And Jumbo was truly a giant African elephant, which Barnum bought from the Royal Zoological Society in London.

Phineas Taylor Barnum acquired such a great reputation for fooling the public that he was given the title the Prince of Humbugs.

H. L. Mencken and the Bathtub Hoax

One of the most far-reaching of all hoaxes is the bathtub spoof perpetrated by Henry Louis (H. L.) Mencken, an American satirical writer and former editor of the *Baltimore Evening Sun*. In 1917, Mencken wrote an article as a joke for the *New York Evening Mail* entitled "A Neglected Anniversary" about the first American bathtub.

Mencken gave the honor of inventing this piece of plumbing to Adam Thompson, described as a wealthy cotton and grain dealer from Cincinnati, Ohio. According to Mencken's article, Thompson conceived the idea in 1842 while on a trip to Europe, where he was fascinated by the British bathtubs introduced into England ten years earlier. Upon returning to America, Thompson built a bathtub of mahogany, lined with sheet lead. Then the "inventor" gave a lavish party to unveil his innovation and encouraged guests to try it out.

MENCKEN OWNS UP THAT HE WAS ONLY SPOOFING ABOUT BATHTUBS

"As a practicing journalist for many years, I have often had close contact with history in the making. I can recall no time or place when what actually occurred was afterward generally known and believed. Sometimes a part of the truth got out, but never all. And what actually got out was seldom clearly understood. Consider, for example, the legends that follow every national convention. A thousand newspaper correspondents are on the scene, all of them theoretically competent to see accurately and report honestly, but it is seldom that two of them agree perfectly, and a month after the convention adjourns the accepted version of what occurred usually differs from the accounts of all of them."

"The American public will swallow anything," says Mencken.

By H. L. MENCKEN

On Dec. 28, 1917, I printed in the New York Evening Mail, a paper now extinct, an article purporting to give the history of the bathtub. This article, I may say at once was a tissue of absurdities, all of them deliberate and most of them obvious. I alleged that the bathtub was unknown in the world until the 40s of the last century, and that it was then invented in Cincinnati. I described how the inventor, in the absence of running water in the town, employed Aframericans to haul it up from the Ohio river in buckets. I told how a tub was put into the White House in the 50s, and how Millard Fillmore took the first presidential bath. I ended by saying that the medical men of the United States unanimously opposed the new invention as dangerous to health, and that laws against it were passed in Massachusetts and Pennsylvania.

This article, as I say, was planned as a piece of spoofing to relieve the strain of war days, and I confess that I regarded it, when it came out, with considerable satisfaction. It was reprinted by various great organs of the enlightenment, and after a while the usual letters began to reach me from readers. Then, suddenly my satisfaction turned to consternation. For these readers, it appeared, all took my idle jocosities with complete seriousness. Some of them, of antiquarian tastes, asked for further light on this or that phase of the subject. Others actually offered me corroboration!

PREPOSTEROUS "FACTS" ACCEPTED AS GOSPEL

But the worst was to come. Pretty soon I began to encounter my preposterous "facts" in the writings of other men. They began to be used by chiro-

dence of the stupidity of medical men. They began to be cited by medical men as proof of the progress of public hygiene. They got into learned journals. They were alluded to on the floor of Congress. They crossed the ocean, and were discussed solemnly in England and on the continent. Finally, I began to find them in standard works of reference. Today, I believe, they are accepted as gospel everywhere on earth. To question them becomes as hazardous as to question the Norman invasion.

And as rare. This is the first time, indeed, that they have ever been questioned, and I confess at once that even I myself, their author, feel a certain hesitancy about doing it. Once more, I suppose, I'll be accused of taking the wrong side for the mere pleasure of standing in opposition. The Cincinnati boomers, who have made much of the boast that the bathtub industry, now running to $200,000,000 a year, was started in their town, will charge me with spreading lies against them. The chiropractors will damn me for blowing up their ammunition. The medical gents, having swallowed my quackery, will now denounce me as a quack for exposing them. And in the end, no doubt, the thing will simmer down to a general feeling that I have once more committed some vague and sinister crime against the United States, and there will be a renewal of the demand that I be deported to Russia.

I recite this history, not because it is singular, but because it is typical. It is out of just such frauds, I believe, that most of the so-called knowledge of humanity flows. What begins as a guess —or, perhaps, not infrequently, as a downright and deliberate lie—ends as a fact and is embalmed in the history

books. One recalls the gaudy days of 1914-1918. How much that was then devoured by the newspaper readers of the world was actually true? Probably not 1 per cent. Ever since the war ended learned and laborious men have been at work examining and exposing its fictions. But every one of those fictions retains full faith and credit today. To question even the most palpably absurd of them, in most parts of the United States, is to invite denunciation as a bolshevik.

So with all other wars. For example, the revolution. For years past American historians have been investigating the orthodox legends. Almost all of them turn out to be blowsy nonsense. Yet they remain in the school history books and every effort to get them out causes a dreadful row and those who make it are accused of all sorts of treasons and spoils. The truth, indeed, is something that mankind, for some mysterious reason, instinctively dislikes. Every man who tries to tell it is unpopular, and even when, by the sheer strength of his case, he prevails, he is put down as a scoundrel.

As a practicing journalist for many years, I have often had close contact with history in the making. I can recall no time or place when what actually occurred was afterward generally known and believed. Sometimes a part of the truth got out, but never all. And what actually got out was seldom clearly understood. Consider, for example, the legends that follow every national convention. A thousand newspaper correspondents are on the scene, all of them theoretically competent to see accurately and report honestly, but it is seldom that two of them agree perfectly, and after a month after the convention

adjourns the accepted version of what occurred usually differs from the accounts of all of them.

I point to the Republican convention of 1920, which nominated the eminent and lamented Harding. A week after the delegates adjourned the whole country believed that Harding had been put through by Col. George Harvey; Harvey himself admitted it. Then other claimants to the honor arose, and after a year or two it was generally held that the trick had been turned by the distinguished Harry M. Daugherty, by that time a salient light in the Harding cabinet. The story began to acquire corroborative detail. Delegates and correspondents began to remember things that they had not noticed on the spot. What got orthodox tale is today, with Daugherty in eclipse, I don't know, but you may be sure that it is full of mysterious intrigue and bold adventure.

What are the facts? The facts are that Harvey had little more to do with the nomination of Harding than I did, and that Daugherty was immensely surprised when good Warren won. The intense heat, and to that alone. The delegates, torn by the savage three-cornered fight between Lowden, Johnson and Wood, came to Saturday morning in despair. The temperature in the convention hall was at least 120 degrees. They were eager to get home. When it became apparent that the leaders could not break the deadlock they ran amuck and nominated Harding, as the one aspirant who had no enemies. If any individual managed the business it was not Harvey or Daugherty, but Myron T. Herrick. But so far as I know Herrick's hand in it has never been mentioned.

I turn to a more pleasant field—that of sport in the grand manner. On July 2, 1921, in the great bowl at Jersey City, the Hon. Jack Dempsey met M. Carpentier, the gallant frog. The sympathy of the crowd was overwhelmingly with M. Carpentier and every time he struck a blow he got a round of applause, even if it didn't land. I had an excellent seat, very near the ring, and saw every move of the two men. From the first moment Dr. Dempsey had it all his own way. He could have knocked out M. Carpentier in the first half of the first round. After that first half he simply waited his chance to do it politely and humanely.

Yet certain great newspapers reported the next morning that M. Carpentier had delivered an appalling wallop in the second round and that Dr. Dempsey had narrowly escaped going out. Others told the truth, but what chance had the truth against that romantic lie? It is believed in to this day by at least 99.99 per cent. of all the boxing fans in Christendom. Carpentier himself, when he recovered from his beating, admitted categorically that it was nonsense, but even Carpentier could make no headway against the almost universal human tendency to cherish what is not true. A thousand years hence schoolboys will be taught that the frog had Dempsey going. It may become in time a religious dogma, like the doctrine that Jonah swallowed the whale. Scoffers who doubt it will be damned to hell.

The moral, if any, I leave to psychopathologists, if competent ones can be found. All I care to do today is to reiterate, in the most solemn and awful terms, that my history of the bathtub, printed on Dec. 28, 1917, was pure bunkcombe. If there were any facts in it they got there, accidentally and against my design. But today the tale is in the encyclopedias. History, said a great American soothsayer, is bunk.

(Copyright, 1926)

H.L. Mencken's article exposing his own historical hoax, "The Invention of the Bathtub in America."

The article continued that in the 1850s President Millard Fillmore took the first Presidential bath when he installed a bathtub in the White House. Anticipating a rousing cheer for his invention, Thompson was surprised to learn that others did not share his enthusiasm. Physicians claimed the bathtub was a public health menace. In Boston, a city ordinance prohibited its use except upon medical advice. The state of Virginia charged a thirty-dollar tax on each bathtub's installation. In Pennsylvania, only two no votes kept the Philadelphia city council from passing a law forbidding the bathtub's use from November to May. "In spite of such public outcry," H. L. Mencken concluded his story, "legislators found it impossible to put the bathtub out of existence."

The public was thoroughly fooled by Mencken's hoax. Reprints of the article were published in leading newspapers and magazines across the United States, in federal government publications, in books on American social history, in advertisements for plumbing companies, and in speeches given by famous politicians, heads of health departments, and owners of plumbing companies.

When Mencken first learned of the public's reaction to his article, he said, "My motive was simply to have some harmless fun in war days. It never occurred to me that it would be taken seriously." He wrote a confession of his spoof entitled "Melancholy Reflections," which appeared in thirty American newspapers:

> Pretty soon . . . my preposterous facts . . . began to be cited by medical men as proof of the progress of public hygiene. . . . They were alluded to on the floor of Congress. . . . Finally I began to find them in standard works of reference.

The *Boston Herald* printed a cartoon beneath the article labeled "The American Public Will Swallow Anything." Yet three weeks later, the *Herald* printed on page one Mencken's original fake bathtub article as a news item. Mencken issued another confession, but the public and newspaper columnists seemed to ignore this confession also, as more articles appeared relating Mencken's bathtub hoax as if it were true.

Some tellers of the bathtub tale even falsified Mencken's false facts. In October, 1936, an article in the *United States News* declared that Dolly Madison established the first bathroom in the White House, which caused a minor scandal, as bathing was considered unhygienic, undemocratic, and close to immorality. Andrew Jackson, the article said, eliminated the bathroom, but Millard Fillmore restored it. In August, 1938, a column in the Cleveland *Plain Dealer* claimed that Eli Whitney, the inventor of the cotton gin, first used the bathtub in America in 1820, when he imported one from England.

On three different occasions, H. L. Mencken had to endure seeing his article reprinted in his own newspaper, the *Baltimore Evening Sun*. The third time occurred in 1942, twenty-five years after Mencken wrote his original bathtub spoof, when the hoax appeared as a news feature called "Bathtub's United States Centennial."

In 1951, *The New Yorker* magazine published a profile on then President Harry Truman, stating, "The President seemed reluctant to let go of his belief" that Millard Fillmore introduced the first bathtub into the White House. President Truman even included this "fact" in his lectures to visitors to the executive mansion.

When H. L. Mencken concluded his fictitious history of the bathtub by saying, "It was impossible to legislate the bathtub out of existence," little did Mencken know that it would also be impossible for *him* to retract, confess, or in any other way remove his practical joke from the minds of Americans.

For the person who is fooled by a hoax, the fun, if any, lies in learning how the hoaxer achieved the deception. Although a book editor might be awed at the ingenuity of the forger, the editor does not laugh when the forger sells the publishing company a phony biography of a famous person for a six-figure advance. Similarly, the relatives of a missing or presumed-dead person might listen with great interest as the impostor explains how he or she fooled them into believing their long-lost kin had returned. Even so, the relatives will not dismiss as "all in the name of fun" the money or treasured objects the impostor may have stolen from them.

No one likes to be fooled, and yet each time a hoax is revealed, there is grudging respect for the person who has been able to fool the experts, at least for a while. We all admire creative genius, and the successful hoaxer is a person whose talents have created a fiction so real that it appears to be fact. The danger for the hoaxer and the victim is that the ability to fool others for fun may be used unethically or illegally to obtain power or profit. Throughout history all kinds of hoaxes have been perpetrated for all kinds of reasons. They teach us how vulnerable we are, and at the same time, they help us learn to be aware and how to think more critically about the world and people in it.

Will the exposure of such forgeries and hoaxes as the Mencken's bathtub anniversary, the Hitler diaries, the Cardiff giant, and the fake Vermeer paintings discourage future forgers from perpetrating more hoaxes? Probably not. As Abraham Lincoln once said, "You may fool all the people some of the time; you can even fool some of the people all of the time; but you can't fool all of the people all the time." As long as human nature remains gullible, there will always be practical jokes, April Fools' tricks, and hoaxes that make headlines.

SUGGESTED FURTHER READING

Chrichton, Robert. *The Great Impostor*. (Random House, 1959).

Cohen, Daniel. *Frauds, Hoaxes and Swindles*. (Watts, 1979).

Davis, Natalie Zemon. *The Return of Martin Guerre*. (Harvard University Press, 1983).

Fay, Stephen, Lewis Chester, and Magnus Linkletter. *Hoax, The Inside Story of the Howard Hughes–Clifford Irving Affair*. (Viking Press, 1972).

Franco, Barbara. "The Cardiff Giant: A Hundred Year Old Hoax," *New York History*, October 1969, pp. 420–440.

Irving, Clifford, and Richard Suskind. *Clifford Irving: What Really Happened*. (Grove Press, 1972).

Kenth, Peter. *Anastasia: The Riddle of Anna Anderson*. (Little Brown, 1983).

Larson, Egon. *The Deceivers*. (Roy Publications, 1966).

MacDougall, Curtis D. *Hoaxes*. (Macmillan, 1940; Dover, 1958, revised).

Moss, Norman. *The Pleasures of Deception*. (Crowell, 1977).

Powell, Donald M. *The Peralta Giant: James A. Reavis and The Barony of Arizona*. (University of Oklahoma Press, 1968).

Readers Digest. *Scoundrels and Scalawags*. (Readers Digest Association, 1968).

Waldrop, Ann. *True or False? Amazing Art Forgeries*. (Hastings House Publishers, 1983).

Winslow, John Hathaway, and Alfred Meyer. "The Perpetrator at Piltdown," *Science 83*, September 1983, pp. 33–43.

INDEX

ABOUT THE AUTHORS

CAROLINE ARNOLD has written more than thirty books for children, including award-winning titles *Animals That Migrate*, a New York Academy of Sciences honor book, and *Pets Without Homes*, a Society of Childrens' Book Writers Golden Kite honor book. Ms. Arnold grew up in Minneapolis, Minnesota, and attended Grinnell College and the University of Iowa. She currently lives in Los Angeles, California, with her husband and two children. She teaches a writing course at UCLA Extension.

HERMA SILVERSTEIN author of *Anti-Semitism* and *Scream Machines*, has written numerous articles and stories which have appeared in *Highlights for Children* and *The Friend* magazines. Her article "Mother Teresa and the Poorest of the Poor" won the Highlights for Children Author Award, and appeared in the December, 1983, issue. Ms. Silverstein obtained a Bachelor of Arts degree from Sophie Newcomb College, and has taught art appreciation to elementary school children. She now lives in Santa Monica, California, with her two sons and three dogs.